I.M. Pei

Der Ausstellungsbau für das Deutsche Historische Museum Berlin
The Exhibitions Building of the German Historical Museum Berlin

Herausgegeben von/Edited by Ulrike Kretzschmar

Mit einer Einleitung von/With an introduction
by Hans Ottomeyer

und Beiträgen von/With contributions
by Ulrike Kretzschmar, Werner Sewing,
Christoph Stölzl und/and Heinrich Wefing

Architekturfotografie von/
Architectural photographs by Ulrich Schwarz

Prestel
Munich · Berlin · London · New York

Inhalt
Contents

Hans Ottomeyer   4   Einleitung
Introduction

Christoph Stölzl   18   Pei-Zauber
Pei Magic

Ulrike Kretzschmar   21   Urban Theatre – I.M. Peis Ausstellungsbau
Urban Theatre – I.M. Pei's Exhibitions Building

Werner Sewing   44   Bewegung und Transparenz
Movement and Transparency

Heinrich Wefing   84   Und ewig lockt der Raum
The Eternal Appeal of Space

Einleitung
Introduction

Hans Ottomeyer

Von allen Bauaufgaben zeichnet sich die eines Museums durch hohen ästhetischen Anspruch bei äußerst disparaten formalen wie inhaltlichen Lösungen aus, welche Museumsbauten in Vergangenheit und Gegenwart charakterisieren und ihr Verständnis verstellen.

Bei genauem Hinsehen sind es drei grundverschiedene Ansätze, welche den Museumsbauten zugrunde liegen. Einer dieser Archetypen ist die Gemälde- und Skulpturengalerie, die als hoher, lang gestreckter Bau mit anstoßenden Reihen von Kabinetten ihre Gültigkeit bis heute bewahrt hat. Der zweite Typus ist das kulturhistorische Museum, das seine adäquate Form darin findet, dass es hinter einer Fassade ein Konglomerat von Räumen ringförmig um einen Innenhof führt und durch wechselnde Raumgestalten eine sinnfällige Abfolge aufbaut und darin den Exponaten gerecht zu werden sucht.

Die jüngste dieser Grundformen dürfte die Ausstellungshalle sein, welche erst in der zweiten Hälfte des 19. Jahrhunderts entstanden ist und sich durch ganz andere Zielsetzungen auszeichnet. Ausstellungshallen – exhibition halls – verbinden den Außenraum mit dem Innenraum durch eine filigrane Glas-Eisen-Konstruktion, die als transparente Wand zwischen dem Außenraum und dem Exponat vermittelt. Es ist kein funktionaler Widerspruch, die Schauräume als innere Schale und als Geschossbau im Innern auszuführen, um die konstanten Bedingungen einer sicheren Bewahrung zu gewährleisten. In der Ausstellungsarchitektur haben sich zwischen den fünfziger Jahren, als man gotisch gefasste Skulpturen noch stolz in großen Glashallen präsentierte, und den achtziger Jahren, die stark von konservatorischen Überlegungen geprägt waren, höchste Anforderungen an den Schutz der Exponate ergeben, die architektonische Konsequenzen haben: geschlossene Raumschalen, welche konstante Temperatur, gleichmäßige Luftfeuchtigkeit, gänzlichen Tageslichtausschluss und größtmögliche Sicherheit schaffen.

Unter diesen, zugegebenermaßen widersprüchlichen Prämissen, entstand der Ausstellungsbau des Deutschen Historischen Museums durch I.M. Pei, welcher die schwierige Bauaufgabe auf einem kleinen Restgrundstück auf eindrucksvolle Weise bewältigte.

4

Among the commissions architects get, designing museums is exceptional in the degree of aesthetic input required, though the disparate attitudes to form and content manifested by museum buildings past and present indicate a wide divergence in museum philosophies.

On a closer look, there would appear to be three radically different approaches to museum design. One of these is the painting and sculpture gallery, a concept which has remained valid to this day as an elongated building with successive rows of display rooms. The second type is the cultural history museum, the most striking feature of which is a facade fronting a conglomerate of rooms arranged round an interior courtyard. The varying designs of the rooms constitute a clear sequence that attempts to do justice to the exhibits.

The most recent of these basic forms must be the exhibition hall, which developed only in the second half of the nineteenth century is notable for quite different objectives. Exhibition halls link exterior with interior by means of filigree structures of glass and iron that function as transparent walls between the exterior world and the exhibits. It is not a functional contradiction to arrange the display rooms as an inner shell with storeys in the interior in order to guarantee constant conditions for secure conservation. In exhibition architecture, in the period between the 1950s – when painted Gothic sculptures were still proudly presented in large glass halls– and the 1980s, when conservation considerations came to the fore, protecting the exhibits became paramount. This had architectural consequences – closed room shells that allow for constant temperatures, even humidity, the total exclusion of daylight and maximum security.

These were the admittedly conflicting premises still prevailing when I.M. Pei came to design his exhibition building for the German Historical Museum. A difficult brief on a small leftover site, Pei mastered it very impressively.

Pei's work is an adjunct to Schlüter and de Bodt's Armoury (Zeughaus) structure of 1695–1706, which accommodates the Museum's permanent displays depicting past centuries of German history, set out

Neben dem Gebäude des Zeughauses (1695–1706) von Schlüter und de Bodt, das in zwei Rundgängen die vergangenen Jahrhunderte deutscher Geschichte darstellt, ist der Ausstellungsbau I.M. Peis der gegebene Ort, um dort im Wechsel temporäre Ausstellung zu zeigen, welche Perspektiven und Verbindungslinien zwischen Gegenwart und Vergangenheit vor Augen führen. Dem wird die lapidare Architektur in besonderer Weise gerecht. Durch Reduktion der Materialien und Einfarbigkeit wird der Ausstellungsbau zu monolither Gestalt konzentriert und reagiert auf Licht und Schatten wie eine monumentale steinerne Skulptur. Darin ist der Bau anderer Architektur unvergleichbar und gewinnt im Innern die spezifische Qualität des „fließenden Raums" (Mies van der Rohe).

Licht- und Schattenarchitektur, welche die Größe ungeteilter Formen betont, ist immer das Resultat monochromer Strukturen.

Diese Architektur hat die besondere Eigenschaft, durch das sich wandelnde Aussehen der Volumen, aufgrund der dynamischen Bewegung des Durchschreitenden den Raumeindruck zu erhöhen und die dritte Dimension und die plastischen Werte der Architektur unmittelbar spürbar werden zu lassen. Die Wirkung der Architektur beruht nicht zuletzt auf der schieren Größe der ungegliederten und ungeschmückten Wände. Das Gewicht liegt aber auf der plastischen Durchgestaltung des Baukörpers und den Lichtvaleurs der großflächigen Oberflächengestaltung. „Die physische Größe ist einer der Hauptgründe des Wertes und der Wirkung von Architektur – La grandeur physique est une des principales causes de la valeur et de l'effet de l'architecture" schrieb Quatremère de Quincy 1838 als Resultat seiner Überlegung zur Ästhetik der Architektur.

Die Fragen: Reduktion – wofür, Minimalismus – weswegen, Beschränkung der Mittel – weshalb erfahren ihre Antworten, wenn sie in diesem Kontext gestellt werden. Der Spannungsbogen zwischen dem Ganzen und der Gestaltung seiner Teile braucht zu seinem Erhalt die Stringenz und Klarheit der architektonischen Elemente.

Die ungeteilte Begeisterung, die bei den Vorbesichtigungen sowohl beim Fachpublikum wie auch den Besuchern deutlich wurde, geht bei der Ausstellungshalle im Wesentlichen von den überraschenden Perspektiven des komplizierten, sich allmählich erschließenden Baukörpers und seiner Glieder aus. Die klare Definition der plastischen Dimensionen durch die eindeutigen, weil groß angelegten Licht- und Schattenflächen macht die Innenarchitektur zu einer Vorschule des

I.M. Pei während eines Besuches im Dezember 2002
I.M. Pei on a visit in December 2002

as a double circuit. As the home of special exhibitions, the new building is the very spot to establish perspectives and visual links between present and past. With its reductive minimalism of materials and monochrome surfaces, it is condensed into a monolith shape that reacts to light and shadow like a monumental stone sculpture. The building is quite unlike any other architecture in this respect, and inside it takes on a specific quality of 'fluid space', to use Mies van der Rohe's term.

The architecture of light and shadow, which the very size of the undivided shapes emphasises, is always the result of monochrome structures. As a consequence of the changing appearance of volumes accompanying the dynamic movement of walking through it, this architecture has the particular quality of heightening the impression of space, tangibly bringing out the third dimension and sculptural values of the architecture. The effect of the architecture depends not least on the sheer size of the plain, undivided walls. Yet the weight is upon the consistent detailed sculptural treatment of the structure throughout and the light values of the large-scale handling of surfaces. 'Physical size is one of the main reasons for the value and effect of architecture' – *la grandeur physique est une des principales causes de la valeur et de l'effet de l'architecture* – wrote Quatremère de Quincy in 1838 in his deliberations on the aesthetics of architecture. The answers to questions as to what reduction is for, why minimalism, and

5

Sehens und zur Vorbereitung für die ästhetischen Wahrnehmungen, welche den Besucher in den Schauräumen erwarten.

Die Jahre der Konzeption, Planung, Ausführung und schließlich Vollendung des großen Baus haben dazu geführt, dass nur Wenige auf der Auftraggeber- und Nutzerseite noch im Amt sind, welche den Bau initiierten.

Kultur ist eine langwierige und fast immer zeitversetzte Aufgabe, die demjenigen, der ein Projekt beginnt und ein Gebäude gründet, selten auf geradem und kurzem Wege die Ergebnisse seiner Mühen bringt. Wir ernten die Früchte, die unlängst gesät und kultiviert wurden. Was man beginnt, denkt man der Zukunft zu. Christoph Stölzl ist es zu danken, dass er die Überzeugungskraft entwickelte, den Bundeskanzler und die zuständigen Ministerien für das Anliegen des Deutschen Historischen Museums zu gewinnen und den Bauauftrag zu erteilen.

Die großen Investitionen in die Zukunft der Geschichtskultur, die Pflege materieller Kultur und des Patrimoniums, erfolgten in der Mitte der neunziger Jahre und zeigen erst jetzt ihre Wirkung. Ob dies die richtige Zeit oder eine Unzeit ist, werden erst die nächsten Jahre erweisen. Der Zeitabschnitt von der Idee 1995 bis zu dem Jahr der Fertigstellung 2003 war ein langer Weg.

Es kommt sehr selten vor, dass Architektur schön ist. Meist ist das Bauen zeitgebunden und überfrachtet mit akademischen Lehren, normativen Ideen, einschränkenden Programmen, rigiden Prinzipien, Ordnungen und in Berlin ganz besonders mit Verordnungen, die einen ganzen Orkus von Genehmigungsbehörden beschäftigen, die in dieser Stadt ihr Recht fordern, nach dem jedes Detail und jede Struktur überprüft und auf die Norm gebracht werden. Das die Gestaltungskraft des Architekten und die Prämissen des Museums dabei nicht zugrunde gingen, verdankt das Deutsche Historische Museum Frau Ulrike Kretzschmar, die von den Anfängen an alle Baufragen koordinierte und zwischen dem Architekturbüro I.M. Pei, dem Bundesamt für Bauwesen und Raumordnung als Bauherren, den Auflagen der Genehmigungsbehörde vermittelnd, das Stück Zukunft für die Wechselausstellungen des Deutschen Historischen Museums gerettet hat.

Es besteht kein Zweifel, dass die Ausstellungshalle des Museums in der zukünftigen Architekturgeschichte des 21. Jahrhunderts auf den ersten Seiten eine Rolle spielt und vermittelnd zwischen den Ideen des 20. Jahrhunderts und den Baugedanken einer neuen Epoche steht. Die tiefe Skepsis, die

what end limiting one's resources serves are found in this building. The link between the whole and the design of its parts needs the stringency and clarity of its architectural features to be perceived.

In the case of the exhibition hall, the unanimous enthusiasm evident among both professionals and visitors during previews comes basically from the surprising perspectives you discover in the complex structure and the details you gradually take in. The sharp definition of the sculptural dimensions by the large-scale (and therefore unambiguous) light and shadow surfaces makes the experience of the interior architecture a visual 'tuning-up' process preparing you for the aesthetic experiences awaiting you in the exhibition rooms.

The long years of designing, planning, building and finally completing the great building meant that very few of those involved in initiating the project on the client and user side are still in office.

Culture is a slow-moving business, almost always involving a time shift and a devious, wearisome path to fruition. It rarely crowns in straightforward fashion the efforts of those that launch the project and lay the foundations. In this case, we are reaping the fruits of seeds sown and nursed along quite recently. What is begun, is intended for the future. We have Christoph Stölzl to thank for his powers of persuasion in winning over the federal chancellor and the relevant ministries to the cause of the German Historical Museum and getting the building commissioned.

The great investment in the future of our history and care of our material culture and heritage was undertaken in the mid-1990s, but the fruits of it are only evident now. Whether this was a good or inopportune moment will only transpire in the coming years. It has been a long road from the first idea in 1995 to completion in 2003.

It is very rare for architecture to be beautiful. Mostly, construction is a matter of fashion. It is overburdened with academic doctrine, pressure to standardise, restrictive programmes, rigid principles, regulations and in Berlin in particular with official directives that keep a whole Stygian underworld of licensing authorities busy demanding their pound of flesh. They check every detail and every structure to see that the rules have been complied with. The German Historical Museum owes it to Ulrike Kretzschmar, who co-ordinated all architectural matters from the first, that the architect's creative power and the museum's

bei der Fachkritik und den Zunftgenossen in Berlin herrscht, ob eine Architektur in qualitativ herausragender Art nicht eine Störung bedeutet, weil sie sich nicht der umgebenden Baulandschaft an- und einpasst, wird durch die Architektur Peis ad absurdum geführt. Die Fassaden antworten, reflektieren und widerstehen den sie umgebenden Stadträumen und Straßen in dialogischen Bezügen. Dabei entstehen neue Perspektiven sowie sorgfältig komponierte Durchblicke und Bilder, die bereits jetzt zu Topoi der Berliner Stadtveduten wurden, wenn man beobachtet, wie Fotografen immer wieder dieselben Standorte und Blickwinkel aufsuchen.

Das Haus dient den Ausstellungen insoweit, wie es zu ihnen führt, den Weg zu ihnen vermittelt und sie zuverlässig birgt. Pei schlägt sehr bewusst die Brücken zwischen dem Außenbereich, dem Foyer und den Ausstellungsräumen tief im Inneren des Gebäudes. Dies ist Funktionalität jenseits eines trivialen Zweckdenkens, das den unmittelbaren Nutzen kalkuliert.

Die Ausstellungshalle Peis steht in einem Umfeld von Kulturbauten, die sich auf verschiedenste Weise definieren: Museen, Theater, Gedenkstätte, Kulturverwaltungen, Universität, Justizgebäude und demnächst ein Galeriebau. Deswegen ist die unverkennbare Gestalt eines Ausstellungsgebäudes eine deutliche Markierung dieser Bestimmung und rechtfertigt das markante Herausstellen des geschossübergreifenden Treppenturms.

Die Eröffnung des Hauses von I.M. Pei ist der entscheidende Schritt für die Zukunft des Deutschen Historischen Museums und erlaubt auf hohem Niveau und in verschränkten Perspektiven die Geschichte Deutschlands im europäischen Kontext zu erörtern. Erst das Zusammengehen von Form und Inhalt bietet die Ausblicke und Einsichten, welche der Geschichte ihre Zukunft konstruieren.

expectations were not permanently beached on this rather inhospitable shore.

She was the intermediary between I.M. Pei's architectural office and the client (the federal construction office) and negotiated the conditions with the licensing authorities, thereby saving this piece of the future for the German Historical Museum's special exhibitions.

There is no doubt that the Museum's exhibition hall will feature in the opening pages of the future architectural history of the twenty-first century, and will act as a bridge between the ideas of the twentieth century and the architectural concepts of a new era.

The profound scepticism predominant among architectural critics and architectural professionals that architecture of quality may represent a disruption because it does not adapt to and fit in with the surrounding built environment, can be perceived as absurd in the context of Pei's architecture. The facades respond to, reflect and resist the urban buildings and streets around them in a kind of dialogue. They open up new vistas and meticulously composed perspectives and images that have already become subject matter for postcards and souvenirs of Berlin, to judge from the number of photographers who constantly seek out these same spots and scenes.

The building serves the exhibitions to the extent that it provides access to them, shows the way to them and houses them appropriately. Pei is very deliberate about the way he builds bridges from the exterior world through the foyer to the exhibition rooms deep inside the building. This is functionality far beyond any trivial utilitarianism that calculates only direct purposes.

Pei's exhibition hall stands in an environment of cultural buildings that reflect a wide range of cultural concerns – museums, theatres, memorials, cultural administrations, the university, law buildings and soon a gallery building. For this reason, the unmistakable shape of an exhibition building is a clear mark of this function and justifies the prominence given to the distinctive stair tower rising out of it.

The opening of Pei's building is a historic moment for the future of the German Historical Museum. It enables the history of Germany to be debated in a European context in an informed way and appropriate perspective. It is the fusion of form and content that offers vistas and insights that lend history its future.

Blick von der Straße Hinter dem Gießhaus auf den Erweiterungsbau
View of the extension from Hinter dem Giesshaus street

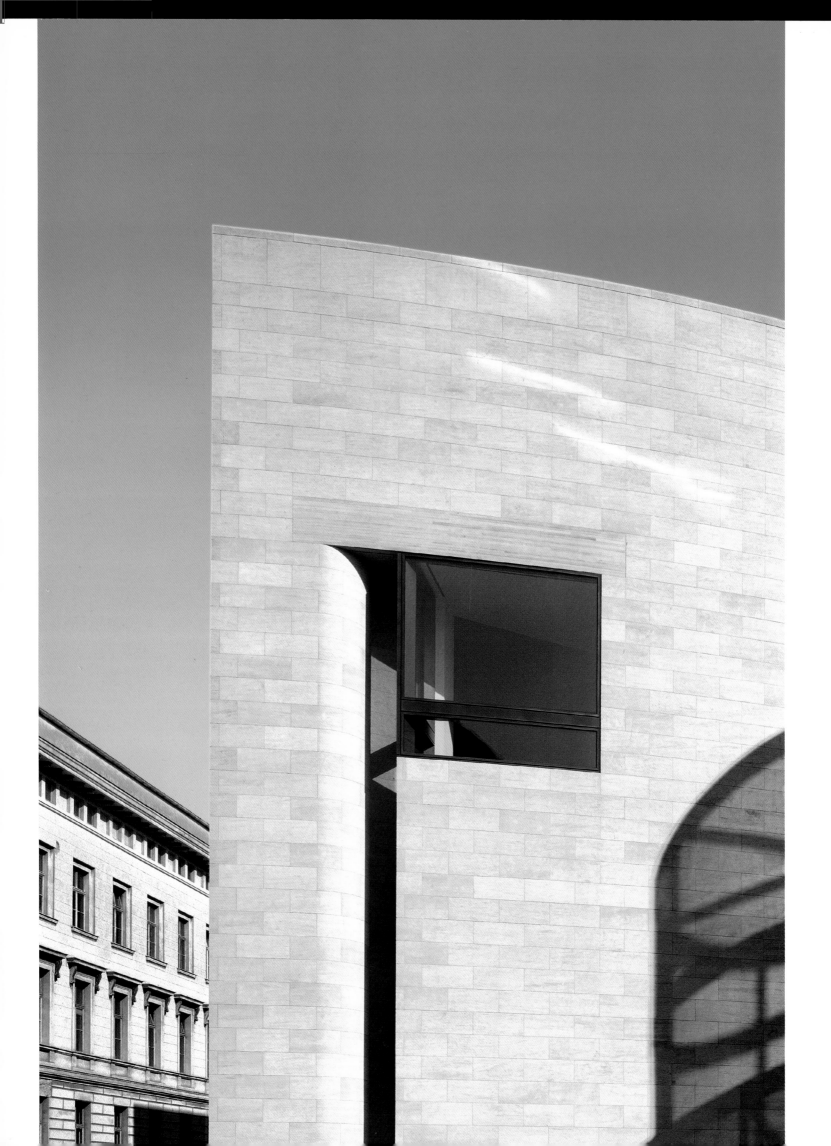

Panoramafenster im zweiten Obergeschoss des Ausstellungsgebäudes
Panoramic window on the second floor of the exhibition building

Eingangssituation von der Straße Hinter dem Gießhaus
Entrance on Hinter dem Giesshaus street

Gläserner Erker an der Rückfront des Ausstellungsgebäudes
Glazed oriel in the rear facade of the exhibition building

Terrasse im zweiten Obergeschoss
Terrace on the second floor

Gläserner Erker an der Rückfront des Ausstellungsgebäudes
Glazed oriel in the rear facade of the exhibition building

Der gläserne Treppenturm mit Blick auf das Palais am Festungsgraben
The glass stairtower with the view of the Palais am Festungsgraben

Blick von der gläsernen Spindel auf die Nordfassade des Zeughauses
View from the glass spiral stairtower towards the north facade of the Armoury

Der überdachte Schlüterhof im Zeughaus

The covered Schlüterhof in the Armoury

Pei-Zauber
Pei Magic

Christoph Stölzl

Kleine Angeln drehen große Türen. An einem Sommernachmittag des Jahres 1995 war in einem Garten in Dahlem ein bürgerlicher Kreis versammelt, gesellig zwecklos, doch den Berliner Sitten folgend, sogleich streitbar in aktuelle Kulturprobleme verwickelt. Wolf Jobst Siedler, Grand Old Man der hauptstädtischen Architekturkritik, beklagte die Schwächen des ungehemmten Baubooms im Herzen der Stadt und meinte resigniert: wie anders, besser, würdiger sähe das neue Berlin aus, wenn die großen Klassiker des Jahrhunderts, wie z.B. I.M. Pei ihre Handschrift hätten hinzufügen können. Aber da sei ja das deutsche Wettbewerbswesen vor, von Pei wisse man schließlich, dass er nur Projekte eigener Wahl annehme. Pei-Erinnerungen, Pei-Schwärmerei, Pei-Kontroversen machten die Runde: Das Für und Wider der Louvre-Pyramide, die doppeldeutige politische Symbolik des Bank of China-Turms in Hongkong. Ohne Widerspruch blieb mein Bekenntnis, dass der Washingtoner East Wing der National Gallery unsere Vorstellung vom perfekten Museum für immer verändert habe: ein Raum, dessen Schönheit so unvergesslich sei, weil in ihm Besucher und Kunstwerke auf magische Weise symbiotisch vereinigt würden. War es der laue märkische Sommerabend oder die Anmut bildungsbürgerlichen Möglichkeitssinns? Jedenfalls war, schon Augenblicke später kaum mehr rekonstruierbar, auf einmal eine utopische Wette da: Würde I.M. Pei den Anbau des Deutschen Historischen Museums bauen, würde Christoph Stölzl eine Kiste Champagner gewinnen – gegen eine Dame, die derlei Utopien für typisches Männer-Gerede hielt.

Am nächsten Tag schrieb Wolf Jobst Siedler an I. M. Pei. Es war ein Brief der self fullfiling prophecy. Denn zu diesem Zeitpunkt gab es weder einen Entschluss der Bundesregierung zum Bau noch ein Budget dafür. Als mich aber, durchaus überraschend, zehn Tage später I. M. Pei anrief und sehr freundlich dazu einlud, einmal hereinzuschauen, wenn mich mein Weg nach New York führe, sagte ich kurzentschlossen, schon fast übermorgen sei dies der Fall. Si non vero, bene trovato – der Pei-Zauber wirkte. Am 21. August begann in der Madison Avenue 600 ein Gespräch über Berlin, Deutschland, deutsche Geschichte, deutsche Architektur, das

Small hinges open large doors. One summer afternoon in 1995, a group of respectable citizens had congregated in a garden in suburban Berlin, not with any end in mind other than conviviality, but as is the way in Berlin, soon in heated argument about current cultural problems. Wolf Jobst Siedler, the doyen of metropolitan architectural critics, lamented the weaknesses of the unchecked building boom in the city centre and commented resignedly how different, better and altogether more dignified the new Berlin would look if great classic architects of the century such as I.M. Pei had been able to add their bit. But German competition rules wouldn't let that happen, after all it was known Pei would only take on work he had chosen himself. Pei anecdotes, Pei enthusiasm and Pei controversy soon followed – pros and contras of the Louvre pyramid, the ambiguous political symbolism of the Bank of China tower in Hong Kong, etc. There was no dissent when I said that the East Wing of the National Gallery in Washington had permanently changed our ideas of the perfect museum – a space whose beauty is so unforgettable because in it visitors and art are symbiotically united in quite magical fashion. Was this all the mild Brandenburg summer air or the educated classes delighting in fanciful speculations? At any rate, just moments later a utopian bet was on the table – if I.M. Pei took on the extension of the German Historical Museum, Christoph Stölzl would win a crate of champagne, from a lady who dismissed such fancies as typical male talk.

The next day Wolf Jobst Siedler wrote to I.M. Pei. The letter was something of a self-fulfilling prophecy, because at that date the Federal government had neither passed a resolution in favour of the extension nor voted a budget for it. When therefore to my great surprise I.M. Pei called me ten days later and very kindly invited me to drop in if my path took me to New York, it was the decision of an instant to say that that would be almost the day after tomorrow. Si non vero, bene trovato – the Pei magic worked. On 21 August, a conversation about Berlin, Germany, German history, German architecture and the Bauhaus (with which both of us have personal connec-

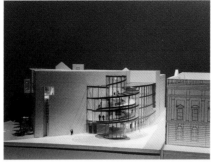

1   2

Bauhaus (dem wir beide biographisch verbunden sind), das viele Stunden dauerte. Es legte den Grundstein zu Peis Engagement für Berlin. Als ich am Nachmittag ins glutheiße Manhattan hinaustrat, wusste ich instinktiv, dass mein Traum wahr werden würde. Pei baut dort, wo er es für notwendig hält, der Same war gesät. Im Herbst kam Pei nach Berlin, betrat wieder seine lebenslange Brücke zu Schinkel, die einst sein Lehrer Gropius gebaut hatte. Zu Fuß das Herz von Berlin durchwandernd, schlug er seinen analytischen Zirkel rund um das Zeughaus. Und entdeckte: Der zukünftige Bauplatz liegt, symbolisch genug, „between the two Schinkels", den Meisterwerken Neue Wache und Altes Museum.

Und dann besuchte Pei Helmut Kohl in Bonn. Denkwürdig das Gespräch im Kanzleramt, die beiden Männer, unterschiedlicher kaum zu denken: Hier der massige Einiger Europas, täglich verstrickt in mühsame Machtpolitik, dort der global agierende zierliche Schöpfer makelloser Gebilde. Die Wechselrede kreist um Mitterand, Paris, die Rolle der Hauptstädte, die Rolle der Kultur in der Weltpolitik. Schließlich der überraschende Griff des Kanzlers nach einer Schublade. Darin verborgen ein Plattenspieler: Es erklingt ein Divertimento von W.A. Mozart. Seltsame, unwirkliche Szene, das Gespräch erlischt. Ich spüre: Die beiden sind sich einig, wortlos. Um den administrativen Rest war mir nicht bang, so merkwürdig das klingt. Der Normalfall des öffent-

tions) got under way at 600 Madison Avenue and went on for several hours. It laid the foundation for Pei's involvement with Berlin. When I stepped out into the fiery heat of Manhattan that afternoon, I knew instinctively that my dream would come true. Pei builds where he thinks it is necessary – the seed was sown. That autumn, he came to Berlin and re-trod the lifelong bridge to Karl Schinkel that his teacher Gropius had once built for him. Wandering through the centre of Berlin on foot, he ran his analytical dividers round the Armoury (Zeughaus). And discovered that the future building site lay symbolically enough 'between the two Schinkels', i.e. his great Neue Wache (New Guardhouse) and Altes Museum (Old Museum) buildings.

Then Pei went to see Helmut Kohl in Bonn. It was a memorable conversation in the Chancellor's Office, between two men who could hardly be more different. On the one hand the sturdy unifier of Germany who spent his days in the intricacies of power politics, on the other the fragile creator of immaculate constructions the world over. The conversation ebbed to and fro over Mitterand, Paris, the role of capitals and the role of culture in world politics. Finally, the chancellor suddenly opened a drawer, revealing a disc-player inside. The sounds of a Mozart divertimento rang out. It was a strange, unreal scene, the conversation died. My sense was that the two

19

1 Papiermodell für die Präsentation am 16.01.1997 · Paper model for the presentation on 16.01.1997

2 Präsentation des Entwurfs durch den Architekten bei Bundeskanzler Dr. Helmut Kohl in Bonn am 16.01.1997 · Presentation of the architectural model to Chancelor Helmut Kohl in Bonn on 16.01.1997

3   4

lichen Bauens ist, dass erst die Aufgabe da ist, der „Bedarf",
die „Nutzfläche", die „Haushaltsanmeldung", die Normen,
die Zwänge – und dann, weit abgeschlagen – der Geist und
die Kunst. Hier war es einmal umgekehrt. Pei, einst erzogen
von dem deutschen Emigranten Walter Gropius im aufge-
klärten Geist Schinkels, schlägt im hohen Alter den Bogen
zu Berlin und kehrt damit zu einer Wurzel seiner Architektur zurück.

Kann es eine notwendigere Figur geben?

Der Rest war mühsam wie alle Politik. Aber dem utopi-
schen Reiz dieses einzigen Entwurfs von Pei für Deutschland
konnte sich am Ende niemand entziehen – nicht Abgeord-
nete, nicht der Finanzminister, nicht Baubehörden, nicht
Denkmalpfleger, nicht Architektenverbände. Selbst partei-
politische Gegensätze hielten dem Pei-Zauber nicht stand:
Im Haushaltsausschuss des Bundestages stimmte die
Opposition dem Regierungsentwurf zu. Zwei Jahre nach
dem Dahlemer Sommerabend wurde die Wette eingelöst.
Und wiederum acht Jahre danach ist das Herz von Berlin
um ein Architekturwunder reicher.

men were in accord, past words. Funnily enough, I had
no fears about the administrative side to come.

In normal cases of public works, the job is there first –
the 'requirement', the 'floor space', the 'budget notifica-
tion', the standards, the constraints – and then, much
lower down, intellect and art. Here it was the other way
round. Once schooled by German emigré Walter Gropius
in the enlightened spirit of Schinkel, Pei in his advanced
years established a link with Berlin and thus returned to
one of the sources of his architecture. Can there be a
more necessary figure?

The rest was hard work, like all politics. But ultimately
no-one was able to deny the utopian charm of this, Pei's
sole design for Germany – neither representatives, nor
finance minister, nor building authorities, nor heritage
bodies nor architectural associations. Even party political
differences could not stop the Pei magic from happening:
the parliamentary opposition agreed to the government's
proposal. Two years after that suburban summer evening,
the bet was won. Eight years later an additional arcitec-
tural wonder has come about in the heart of Berlin.

3   Der erste Spatenstich am 27.08.1998 in Anwesenheit des Bundeskanzlers Dr. Helmut Kohl und des Architekten · Cutting the first sod on
27.08.1998 with Chancelor Helmut Kohl and the architect

4   Rede I.M. Peis zur Festveranstaltung anlässlich des ersten Spatenstichs ·
I.M.Pei giving a speech on the occasion of the first sod being cut on
27.08.1998

Urban Theatre – I.M. Peis Ausstellungsbau
Urban Theatre – I.M. Pei's Exhibitions Building

Ulrike Kretzschmar

Mit der feierlichen Eröffnung des von dem Architekten Ieoh Ming Pei entworfenen, nördlich des Zeughauses gelegenen Wechselausstellungsgebäudes im Mai 2003 geht die langjährige und wechselvolle Planungszeit des Deutschen Historischen Museums erfolgreich zu Ende. Politischer Widerstand gegen das Projekt eines nationalen Geschichtsmuseums in Berlin, der Fall der Mauer im November 1989 und eine Verlagerung des geplanten Standortes kennzeichnen die über 16 Jahre dauernde Planungs- und Baugeschichte des Deutschen Historischen Museums: Von einer geradlinigen Entwicklung, die direkt von der Idee zum fertigen Gebäude geführt hätte, kann hier nicht die Rede sein.

Die Bundesrepublik Deutschland und das Land Berlin unterzeichneten am 28. Oktober 1987, anlässlich der 750-Jahr-Feier der Stadt Berlin, im Reichstagsgebäude die Gründungsvereinbarung für die Einrichtung des Deutschen Historischen Museums. Zu diesem Zeitpunkt war für das neue Museum noch ein ganz anderer Bauplatz vorgesehen. Kaum ein kulturpolitisches Vorhaben der Bundesrepublik Deutschland hat so viele heftige und kontroverse Debatten in der Fachwelt und in der Presse ausgelöst wie der Plan, in West-Berlin ein historisches Museum zu bauen. Diese Debatten bezogen sich auf Konzeption und Standortwahl gleichermaßen. Das von Bundeskanzler Dr. Helmut Kohl ins Leben gerufene Geschichtsmuseum ist eine von drei Kulturinstitutionen, die der Bund in den achtziger Jahren gründete. Es sollte das westliche Pendant zu dem seit 1952 bestehenden Museum für Deutsche Geschichte im damaligen Ost-Berlin sein und zugleich das in Bonn geplante Haus der Geschichte der Bundesrepublik ergänzen.

Noch bevor erste konzeptionelle Überlegungen angestellt wurden oder der Name festgestanden hätte, war die Idee eines Geschichtsmuseums in Berlin eng mit der Diskussion über ein geeignetes historisches Gebäude in der Stadt verbunden. Keines der Häuser, die damals in Erwägung gezogen wurden – etwa der Martin-Gropius-Bau, die Zitadelle Spandau, der Reichstag oder die Kongresshalle –, stand jedoch wirklich zur Verfügung oder war für das Projekt geeignet. Mit dem Entschluss der Bundesregierung, einen Neubau zu finanzieren, fiel im Sommer 1986 auch die

With the festive opening of Ieoh Ming Pei's special exhibitions building north of Schlüter's Armoury in Berlin in May 2003, years of planning and turbulence in the development of the German Historical Museum finally reached a successful conclusion. Political resistance to the project for a national historical museum in Berlin, the fall of the Wall in November 1989 and relocation of the planned site were among the vicissitudes of the museum's sixteen-year planning and building history. Its completion was certainly no simple matter of going in a straight line directly from the idea to the finished building.

The foundation agreement setting up the Historical Museum was signed in the Reichstag by the Federal government and the State government of Berlin on 28 October 1987, the day the city of Berlin celebrated the 750th anniversary of its founding. At the time, a wholly different location was planned for the new museum. Scarcely any cultural project of the Federal Republic aroused such fierce controversy in the professional world and the press as the plan to build a historical museum in West Berlin. The argument involved both the scheme itself and the choice of location. The historical museum was a government initiative, one of three cultural institutions founded by the federal government in the 1980s. It was supposed to be the western counterpart to the Museum for German History founded in 1952 in what was then East Berlin, and also a complement to a planned museum for the history of the Federal Republic in Bonn.

Even before the first detailed proposals had been roughed out or the name settled, the idea of a historical museum in Berlin had been closely linked with the discussion about a suitable historic building in the city. None of the buildings considered then – for example the Martin Gropius Building, Spandau Citadel, the Reichstag or the Congress Hall – were really available or suited to the project. So when the federal government in 1986 opted for a new building, the location was also settled – in a bend of the Spree, opposite the Reichstag.[1] A site with a total area of 36,000 m² was set aside for the implementation of the newly founded museum.

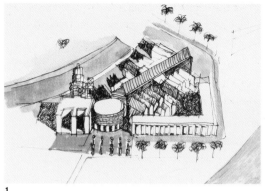 

1   2

Entscheidung für den Standort: im Spreebogen, gegenüber dem Reichstag.[1] Für die Realisierung des neu zu gründenden Museums war damals eine Gesamtfläche von rund 36.000 m² Hauptnutzfläche vorgesehen.

Anlässlich des Ausgabekolloquiums im Architektenwettbewerb am 25. August 1987 bezeichnete Bauminister Dr. Oscar Schneider den Bau des Deutschen Historischen Museums als „eine der verantwortungsvollsten und reizvollsten Aufgaben, zu denen wir bis zum Ende dieses Jahrhunderts einladen können".[2]

Den Wettbewerb gewann im Juni 1988 der Mailänder Architekt Aldo Rossi (1931–1997). Er entwarf für den Spreebogen eine ganze Anthologie alteuropäischer Architekturformen – Kolonnade, Turm, Basilika, Rotunde – als eine zusammenhängende Museumslandschaft.

Die heftige Kontroverse um das Vorhaben „Deutsches Historisches Museum" hielt weiter an. Als nach den Berliner Wahlen im Januar 1989 ein Regierungswechsel stattfand, wurde das Kulturprojekt der Bundesregierung in den Koalitionsverhandlungen unversehens zum Politikum. Unterstützung kam jedoch von Seiten des ehemaligen Bundeskanzlers und SPD-Vorsitzenden Willy Brandt, der sich

On the occasion of the launch of the architectural competition on 25 August 1987, Construction Minister Oscar Schneider described the construction of the German Historical Museum as 'one of the most responsible and attractive tasks we can issue invitations for up to the end of this century.'[2]

The competition was won in June 1988 by the Milanese architect Aldo Rossi (1931–97). His scheme for the Spree Bend was a whole anthology of established European architectural features – with a colonnade, tower, basilica, rotunda – as a connected museum landscape.

Nonetheless, the heated controversy about the proposed German Historical Museum refused to go away. When the elections of January 1989 brought a change of government in Berlin, the federal government's cultural project suddenly became a political issue in coalition negotiations. However, former federal chancellor and SPD chairman Willy Brandt lent his whole-hearted support to the scheme. In a letter of congratulation to the newly elected mayor, he said he did not think it desirable for Berlin to exclude itself from a project that had attracted so much international interest.[3]

The fall of the Wall in November 1989 put a stop to discussions for the time being, and basically changed all the plans that had been worked out up to that point. At the end of August 1990, the East German government decided not to go on with the Museum for German History housed in the Armoury (Zeughaus) as an independent body, and the following month abandoned it. Following reunification on 3 October 1990, the Armoury and its collections were handed over to the German Historical Museum on a temporary basis. This handover made the museum the first pan-German cultural institution to be set up.

22

1   Aldo Rossi, Entwurfszeichnung für das Deutsche Historische Museum in West-Berlin, 1988 · Aldo Rossi, design for the German Historical Museum in West Berlin, 1988

2   Aldo Rossi, Modell für das Deutsche Historische Museum in West-Berlin, 1988 · Aldo Rossi, architectural model of the German Historical Museum in West Berlin, 1988

3   I.M. Pei, Modell für das Wechselausstellungsgebäude des Deutschen Historischen Museums, 1997 · I.M. Pei, architectural model of the Special Exhibitions Building for the German Historical Museum

eindeutig für das Deutsche Historische Museum aussprach. In seinem Gratulationsschreiben an den neuen Regierenden Bürgermeister hielt er es „*nicht für wünschenswert, wenn Berlin sich von diesem Vorhaben, auf das sich auch das internationale Interesse konzentriert, ausschlösse*".[3]

Der Mauerfall im November 1989 unterbrach die Diskussionen bis auf weiteres und veränderte alle bis dahin erarbeiteten Pläne von Grund auf. Bereits Ende August 1990 beschloss die Regierung der DDR, das im Zeughaus befindliche Museum für Deutsche Geschichte „*nicht als selbständige Einheit fortzuführen*" und gab die Institution im September 1990 auf. Mit dem Tag der Wiedervereinigung am 3. Oktober 1990 wurden das Zeughaus und seine Sammlungen dem Deutschen Historischen Museum zur temporären Nutzung übergeben. Diese Zusammenlegung machte das Museum zur ersten gesamtdeutschen Kultureinrichtung. Nach dem Hauptstadtbeschluss von 1991, der den Umzug der Regierung von Bonn nach Berlin vorsah, stand 1992 endgültig fest, dass an eine Realisierung des Rossi-Baus am geplanten Standort nicht zu denken war. Heute befindet sich auf dem dafür vorgesehenen Bauplatz am Spreebogen das Bundeskanzleramt der Architekten Axel Schultes und Charlotte Frank. Schultes hatte 1988 den dritten Preis des Museumswettbewerbes gewonnen.

Die Räumlichkeiten, die das Zeughaus bot, entsprachen nicht dem ursprünglichen Raum- und Funktionsplan, der in den Jahren 1985 bis 1987 von einer Sachverständigenkommission für das Projekt entwickelt worden war. Das wissenschaftlich begründete Konzept des Deutschen Historischen Museums hatte allein für die Dauerausstellung 16.000 m² und für die Wechselausstellung 5.000 m² gefordert. Eine Reduktion auf das im Zeughaus-Komplex Machbare war unumgänglich. Museum und Sachverständigenkommission akzeptierten die notwendige Verringerung auf etwa die Hälfte des ursprünglich geforderten Raumprogramms.

Der neue Standort im Herzen Berlins, an der Prachtstraße Unter den Linden, vis-à-vis der Museumsinsel, wog jedoch alle Einschränkungen auf. Das historische Zeughaus mit seiner Ausstellungsfläche von ca. 7.500 m² war nun für die zukünftige Dauerausstellung vorgesehen. Für die benötigten Wechselausstellungsflächen sollte ein neues Gebäude mit unmittelbarer Verbindung zum Hauptgebäude geschaffen werden. Platz hierfür bot allein das an das Zeughaus angrenzende Grundstück, auf dem Ende der fünfziger Jahre die Depot- und Werkstattgebäude des Museums für Deutsche Geschichte errichtet worden waren.[4]

Once the government had decided in 1991 to move the seat of government from Bonn to Berlin, it finally became clear by 1992 that implementing the Rossi scheme in the planned location was a non-starter. Today, the earmarked site in the bend of the Spree is occupied by Axel Schultes and Charlotte Frank's Federal Chancellery. Schultes had come third in the 1988 museum competition.

The premises the Armoury offered were irreconcilable with the original plan for the use and arrangement of the museum as drawn up for the project by a committee of experts before 1985. A scheme based on scholarly principles, it foresaw 16,000 m² of permanent exhibition space for the German Historical Museum and 5,000 m² for special exhibitions. Scaling the proposals down to the space available in the Armoury complex was therefore unavoidable. The Museum and a committee of experts agreed to cut the scheme back to about half the size of the original.

The new location in the heart of Berlin, opposite Museum Island on the grand Unter den Linden avenue, was compensation for all the limitations. The historic Armoury building with an exhibition area of about 7,500 m² was now earmarked for the future permanent exhibition. The special exhibitions rooms would require a new building directly linked to the main building. The only space available for this was the site bordering the Armoury, where a depository and workshop building had been constructed for the Museum of Germany History in the late 1950s.[4]

The difficult business of turning a small, awkward plot of land into an attractive place located between two prominent Schinkel buildings – the Neue Wache and

23

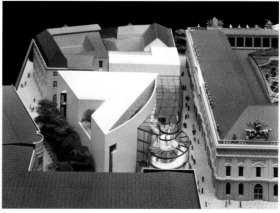

3

Für die schwierige Aufgabe, ein kleines und versteckt ge-
legenes Grundstück in einen attraktiven Ort zu verwandeln,
der sich zwischen zwei prominenten Schinkelbauten – der
Neuen Wache und dem Alten Museum – sowie dem Zeughaus, dem einzigen erhaltenen profanen Barockgebäude
Berlins souverän behaupten würde, konnte die Bundesrepublik den Architekten I.M. Pei gewinnen.

Berühmt wurde der sino-amerikanische Architekt in den
siebziger und achtziger Jahren durch seine meisterliche
Verbindung von Alt und Neu: Mit dem Anbau an die National
Gallery in Washington, mit dem Museum of Fine Arts in
Boston und vor allem mit seinem großartigen Entwurf für die
Erweiterung und Renovierung des Grand Louvre in Paris
stellte er sein geniales Können unter Beweis. Peis Fähigkeit,
für seine Bauten eine dem jeweiligen Ort angemessene
Sprache zu finden und eben nicht nur durch eine „typische
Handschrift" aufzufallen, machte ihn zum idealen Archi-
tekten auch für das Deutsche Historische Museum.

Seit er Ende 1990 aus seiner Firma Pei, Cobb, Freed &
Partners ausschied, nimmt er nur noch wenige ausgesuchte
Projekte an. Mit einem Lächeln und Augenzwinkern verweist
Pei stets auf sein Alter, um sein wählerisches Verhalten zu
begründen. Die erste Kontaktaufnahme mit dem Büro von
I.M. Pei erfolgte Anfang Mai 1995. Auf die Frage, ob er sich
vorstellen könne, in Berlin ein Museum zu bauen, reagierte
er interessiert, aber auch zurückhaltend. Im Herbst kam es
dann zu einem ersten Treffen mit dem damaligen Bundeskanzler Dr. Helmut Kohl. Das gemeinsame intensive Gespräch über die Probleme der neuen Hauptstadt Berlin beein-
druckte I.M. Pei nachhaltig. Wie schon vor seinem Ja zum
Louvre-Projekt, zog er in den kommenden Monaten systema-
tisch Erkundungen über die Bauaufgabe sowie über das
architektonische und politische Umfeld ein. Erst danach
wollte er eine definitive Antwort geben. Mehrmals besuchte
Pei in dieser Zeit Berlin – zweimal sogar „inkognito", da er
ungestört und unbeeinflusst von den Kommentaren anderer
sein wollte, um sich ein persönliches Bild vom Standort und
der damit verbundenen Aufgabenstellung zu machen. Dabei
erkannte er die „Schlüsselrolle" des Platzgefüges Neue
Wache – Kastanienwäldchen – Zeughaus – Inselbrücke –
Museumsinsel. Dieses Ensemble, so seine tiefste Überzeugung, könne für den flanierenden Fußgänger zu einer un-
vergleichlichen Attraktion werden. Pei war bereit, diese
Herausforderung anzunehmen.

Am 26. Juni 1996 gab der Haushaltsausschuss des
Deutschen Bundestages seine Zustimmung zu einem Neubau

Altes Museum – and the Armoury, the only surviving
Baroque secular building in Berlin, was entrusted by the
Federal government to I.M. Pei.

The Chinese-born American architect had become
famous in the museum world in the 1970s and 1980s for
his masterly combinations of new and old. His work at the
National Gallery in Washington, the Museum of Fine Arts
in Boston and above all his splendid design for the extension and renovation of the Grand Louvre in Paris were
adequate demonstration of his genius for this kind of
work. Pei's uncanny ability to find an idiom for his buildings appropriate to the given site rather than score with
a 'typical' style of his own made him the ideal architect
for the German Historical Museum.

Since retiring from his company, Pei, Cobb, Freed
and Partners, at the end of 1990, Pei has taken on only
a few selected projects. With a smile and twinkle in his
eye, he always cites his age as an explanation for his
pickiness.

The first contact with his office came in early May 1995.
When asked if he could imagine building a museum in
Berlin, he reacted with interest but also reserve. Then in
the autumn, he had a first meeting with the then Federal
Chancellor, Helmut Kohl. The highly focused conversation
about the problems of Berlin as the new capital made a
lasting impression on Pei. Just as he did before agreeing
to take on the Louvre project, he spent months systematically studying the construction job itself and the political
and architectural environment. Only when he had done
this would he give a definite answer.

Pei visited Berlin several times during this period – twice
even incognito, as he did not want to be interrupted and
influenced by other people's commentaries while he was
familiarising himself with the location and the nature of
the job. This was when he came to appreciate the key
role of the existing topography – Schinkel's Neue Wache,
the wood of chestnut trees, the Armoury, the bridge to
Museum Island and the Island itself. It was, he was
profoundly convinced, a sequence that could become an
incomparable attraction for a strolling pedestrian. Pei
was ready to accept this challenge.

On 26 June 1996, the Bundestag's budget committee
gave its consent to the construction of a new special
exhibitions building for the German Historical Museum,
and made the necessary funds available. The direct
appointment of Pei was expressly welcomed.

für die Wechselausstellungen des Deutschen Historischen Museums und stellte die erforderlichen Mittel bereit. Die direkte Beauftragung I.M. Peis wurde ausdrücklich begrüßt.

Der aufwändigen Prozedur eines Wettbewerbes, wie er bei öffentlichen Bauten zwar nicht zwingend vorgeschrieben, aber üblich ist, hätte sich Pei auch keinesfalls unterworfen. Schon lange beteiligt er sich nicht mehr an Auslobungen. Auch die Aufträge für seine spektakulärsten Museumsbauten – in Paris, in Washington und in Shigaraki/Kyoto, wo er das Miho Museum erbaute – waren Direktaufträge.

Sein Hauptmotiv für die Übernahme der Aufgabe war nicht allein die große Wertschätzung für den Architekten Schinkel, dessen Detailgenauigkeit für I.M. Peis eigene Werke beispielhaft wirkt, und der Umstand, dass sich zwei seiner Bauten in unmittelbarer Nähe des Baugrundes befinden, sondern vor allem die Tatsache, dass Pei in der neuen Hauptstadt des wiedervereinigten Deutschlands arbeiten konnte. Während der Planungsarbeit für den Neubau führten wir in seinem New Yorker Büro viele Gespräche miteinander, in denen er sich sehr für die Ereignisse im November 1989, für die Wiedervereinigung und das Zusammenwachsen von Ost- und West-Deutschland interessierte.

Besonders aufmerksam verfolgte er die Auseinandersetzungen über die „offenen Vermögensfragen", in denen es vor allem um die Rückgabe von Grundstücken bzw. die Entschädigung von Alteigentümern ging. Pei sah hier Parallelen zu seinem persönlichen Leben: Er selbst hatte sich in den vorangegangenen Jahren immer wieder erfolglos bemüht, das großväterliche Anwesen in Suzhou/China mit seinem prächtigen Garten für die Familie zurückzugewinnen. Dieses war von den Kommunisten im Zuge der Bodenreform enteignet worden. Heute ist das Anwesen ein öffentlicher Park.

Bei einem unserer zahlreichen Gespräche stellte ich ihm die Frage, warum er eigentlich vornehmlich im Ausland und nur noch selten in Amerika arbeite. Er antwortete darauf, dass er die Geschichte und Eigenheiten Amerikas kenne. Ihn interessiere bei einem Auftrag nicht allein der Bau mit seiner Funktion und seiner Einbindung in die Umgebung, sondern auch die politische Geschichte des Auftraggeberlandes und die Mentalität der dort lebenden Menschen. Für Pei wird der Entwurf eines Gebäudes so im wahrsten Sinne des Wortes zu einem „Gesamtkunstwerk". Diese analytische Herangehensweise, bei der er stets bestrebt ist, Zeit, Ort und Zweck in eine ideale Balance zu bringen, bestimmt den persönlichen Stil seiner Arbeiten.

Though the costly procedure of a competition is not compulsory for public buildings, it is customary – but Pei would not have taken part under any circumstances. He has long ceased to go in for prize competitions. The commissions for his most spectacular museum buildings – in Paris, Washington and Shigaraki in Kyoto, where he built the Miho Museum – were likewise direct appointments. His main motive for accepting the job now was not just his great esteem for Schinkel and his great attention to detail as well as his two buildings in direct proximity of our site, but principally the fact that he was able to work in the new capital of a reunited Germany. During the planning for the building we had numerous conversations in his New York office, in the course of which he asked about the events in November 1989, re-unification and how East and West Germany were growing together.

He was particularly attentive to the debate about the 'public property' issue, which revolved around the return of land or compensation for previous owners. Here Pei saw parallels with his own life. In past years, he himself had many times endeavoured without success to get back his grandfather's estate in Suzhou (China) with its splendid garden, which had been confiscated by the Communists under land reform. The estate is now a public park.

In one of these many conversations, I asked him why he worked mostly abroad and rarely in America. His answer was that he knew the history and qualities of America. When he took on a job, he was interested not just in the building, what it was for and how it fitted into the setting, but also the political history of the commissioning country and mentality of the people who lived there. Thus for Pei, designing a building is truly an integral, almost holistic matter. This analytical procedure, involving a perennial attempt to establish an ideal balance of time, place and function, is what characterises the personal style of his works.

The commission for the German Historical Museum in Berlin brought Pei back to his roots in classic modernism. It was also his first commission in Germany, in the city that his teachers Walter Gropius and Marcel Breuer left a lasting mark on. It was in one sense a full circle. In 1934, the seventeen-year-old Pei left China to begin his training in America. After a brief spell at the University of Pennsylvania in Philadelphia, he went to the Massachusetts Institute of Technology (MIT) in Boston to study civil engineering, only to switch to architecture shortly afterwards.

Mit dem Auftrag für das Deutsche Historische Museum in
Berlin kehrt I.M. Pei zurück zu den Wurzeln der klassischen
Moderne. Auch baut er zum ersten Mal in Deutschland, in
der Stadt, die seine Lehrer Walter Gropius und Marcel Breuer
wesentlich prägte. Für ihn schließt sich damit gewisserma-
ßen ein Kreis: 1934 verließ Pei als 17-Jähriger China, um in
Amerika seine Ausbildung zu beginnen. Nach einer kurzen
Zeit an der University of Pennsylvania in Philadelphia ging er
1935 an das Massachusetts Institute of Technology (MIT) in
Boston und studierte zunächst Bauingenieurwissenschaften;
bald darauf wechselte er zur Architektur. In den ersten
Jahren seines Studiums beschäftigte er sich intensiv mit Le
Corbusier, weil er in dessen Arbeiten den notwendigen
Wandel der Architektur von der Welt der traditionellen
Schönen Künste hin zur Moderne verwirklicht sah. Von
Le Corbusier bezog er wichtige Inspirationen für etwas
Neues. Pei erinnert sich an ihre erste persönliche Begeg-
nung: *„Ich werde Le Corbusiers Besuch im MIT im November
1936 nicht vergessen, schwarz gekleidet und mit seiner
dicken Brille. Die zwei Tage mit Le Corbusier, oder 'Corbu'
wie wir ihn nannten, waren vielleicht die wichtigsten Tage
in meiner Architektenausbildung."* [5] 1942 setzte Pei sein
Architekturstudium an der Harvard Graduate School of
Design fort, wo er auf Walter Gropius und Marcel Breuer
traf. Der Bauhaus-Gründer Gropius war dort im Jahr 1938
Direktor geworden und hatte eine Gruppe von Architekten
und Künstlern der Bauhaus-Schule mitgebracht. Mit Breuer

5

4

In the first years of study he focused on Le Corbusier,
because he saw his works as implementing the necessary
transformation of architecture from the world of the
traditional fine arts to modernism. In Le Corbusier, he
found substantial inspiration for something new. Pei
recalled their first personal encounter: 'I cannot forget
Le Corbusier's visit to MIT in November 1935, dressed
in black, with his thick glasses. The two days with Le
Corbusier, or "Corbu" as we called him, were probably
the most important days in my architectural education.' [5]
In 1942, Pei moved to the Harvard Graduate School of
Design to continue his architectural studies, where he
met Walter Gropius and Marcel Breuer. Bauhaus founder
Gropius had become its director in 1938, and brought
with him a group of architects and artists from the
Bauhaus. Pei and Breuer became very good friends and
remained so until Breuer's death in 1981.

As his thesis for Gropius in 1946, Pei did his first museum design. The subject was a two-storey art museum in
Shanghai. It was the first of a whole series of museum
buildings he would design during his career. Gropius described this draft design for Shanghai as the best student
thesis that his master classes had ever produced. It 'clearly
shows that an able designer can very well hold on to basic
traditional features – which he has found are still alive –
without sacrificing a progressive conception of design.' [6]

Equally close to Far Eastern tradition and western
modernism, Pei adopted the strict objectivity of the
Bauhaus in his later works but further developed it with
elegant shapes. He is considered today the consummator
of classic modernism.

The initial outcry in professional circles over the
award of a public building job without a prior competition

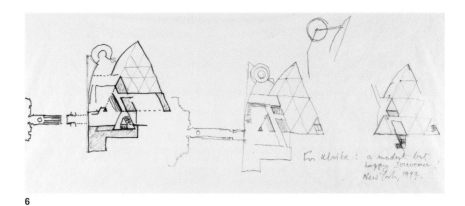

6

verband Pei bis zu dessen Tod im Jahr 1981 eine sehr enge Freundschaft.

Für seine Abschlussarbeit bei Walter Gropius erarbeite Pei 1946 seinen ersten Museumsentwurf. Als Thema wählte er ein zweistöckiges Kunstmuseum in Shanghai. Dies war der Auftakt zu einer ganzen Reihe von Museumsbauten, die er seither gestaltete. Gropius bezeichnete diesen ersten Entwurf für Shanghai als die beste Studentenarbeit, die jemals in seiner Meisterklasse erbracht wurde. „*Sie zeigt deutlich, dass ein fähiger Entwerfer an grundlegenden Traditionen festhalten kann, ohne eine progressive Konzeption des Entwurfes zu opfern.*"[6]

I.M. Pei, dem fernöstliche Tradition und westliche Moderne gleichermaßen nahe stehen, hat in seinen späteren Werken die strenge Sachlichkeit des Bauhauses übernommen, sie zugleich jedoch mit eigenen Formen weiterentwickelt. Er gilt heute als Vollender der klassischen Moderne.

Die anfängliche Kritik der Fachwelt an der Vergabe eines öffentlichen Gebäudes ohne vorangegangenen Wettbewerb verstummte schnell, als I.M. Pei der Öffentlichkeit am 17. Januar 1997 seinen Entwurf vorstellte. Pei hatte mit seiner ersten Präsentation viel erreicht: die Zustimmung der Denkmalpfleger wie auch die der Befürworter moderner Architektur in alter Umgebung.

„*Pei's Entwurf fügt sich in das kleinmaßstäbliche Straßenraster hinter dem Zeughaus ein, aber bildet dennoch mit großer Eleganz einen völlig eigenständigen Kristallkörper, der ohne historisierende Ansprechungen auskommt*"[7] und „*Pei, als Magier des Raumes gepriesen, ist es in Berlin gelungen, Alt und Neu sensibel zusammenzufügen und eine abseitige Restfläche zum Blickfang zu adeln*"[8], so urteilte die Presse begeistert.

Pei verstand es, die Enge des Grundstückes sowie die strikten Auflagen der Denkmalpflege – deutliche Unterordnung in

quickly died away when Pei presented his design to the public on 17 January 1997. He achieved much with his first presentation: the consent of the conservationists and approval of advocates of modern architecture in old environments.

'Pei's design fits into the small-scale street pattern behind the Armoury, but nonetheless constitutes a highly elegant, wholly autonomous crystalline entity devoid of any historicising features'[7], and 'lauded as a conjurer of space, Pei has managed in Berlin to fit old and new together sensitively and ennoble a bit of leftover land into an eye-catcher'[8], were two enthusiastic press comments.

Pei's knack was to transform the limitations of the plot and turn to advantage the strict conditions imposed by the conservationists (e.g. to build perceptibly lower than the Armoury, to preserve perspectives from Mollergasse and Hinter Dem Zeughaus streets behind the Armoury) arising from the sensitive proximity of the surrounding historic buildings. The fact that the new building had few display fronts for facades and moreover a lot of useful space had to be found within it was a further challenge. With a total

4   Zeichnung von Paul Stevenson Oles für die Präsentation des Entwurfs am 16.01.1997 · Drawing by Paul Stevenson Oles for the presentation of the design on 16.01.1997

5   Präsentation des Entwurfs am 17.01.1997 in Berlin in Anwesenheit des Regierenden Bürgermeisters Eberhard Diepgen und des Bundesbauministers Klaus Töpfer · Presentation of the design to the Mayor of Berlin, Eberhard Diepgen, and the minister of the Department of Building, Klaus Töpfer, on 17.01.1997

6   Entwurfszeichnung von I.M. Pei, 1997 · Architectural drawing by I.M. Pei, 1997

7

28

der Bauhöhe gegenüber dem Zeughaus, Bewahrung der
Sichtachsen von Mollergasse und Straße Hinter dem Zeughaus –, die aus der sensiblen Nachbarschaft zu den umliegenden historischen Gebäuden resultierten, in einen Vorzug
umzuwandeln. Die Tatsache, dass der Neubau nur wenige
Schauseiten für Fassaden aufweisen kann und in ihm zudem
viel Nutzfläche untergebracht werden musste, war eine weitere Herausforderung. Pei wählte für das nur knapp 2.000 m²
große Grundstück einen in seiner Grundform als Dreieck
beschriebenen Baukörper, dessen geometrische Strenge
durch eine geschwungene, nach Südwesten vorgelagerte
Wandscheibe gelockert wird. Zwischen Ausstellungsbau und
Zeughaus vermittelt ein beinahe gebäudehohes Glasfoyer,
aus dessen geschwungener Fassade sich ein gläserner
Treppenturm als Blickfang entwickelt.

Das Gebäude mit seinen 4.700 m² Nutzfläche beherbergt
im 1. UG, das gesamte Baugrundstück ausnutzend, den
Hauptausstellungsraum. In den darüber liegenden drei
Etagen befinden sich weitere Präsentationsräume unterschiedlicher Größe und Höhe, so dass auf insgesamt ca.
2.600 m² Fläche maximal vier verschiedene Ausstellungs-
themen gezeigt werden können. Ein kleines Auditorium
mit 57 Plätzen, ein Museumsladen, mehrere kleine Werk-
statträume sowie ein komplettes 2. UG für Zwischendepot
und Technikbereiche runden das Raumprogramm ab.

Dass das im Januar 1997 vorgestellte Modell sowie die anlässlich des ersten Spatenstiches am 27. August 1998 präsentierte Computersimulation nicht zu viel versprachen, konn-
ten Fachpublikum und Öffentlichkeit bereits vier Jahre später
beim Richtfest am 16. April 2002 mit eigenen Augen sehen.

Transparenz, Bewegung und Licht sind die Mittel, mit
denen I.M. Pei das Gebäude zum öffentlichen Ort macht:

plot of barely 2,000 m², Pei opted for a basic building
shape described as a triangle, whose geometrical severity
is softened by a curved wall in front on the south-west
side. An almost full-height glass foyer acts as a link
between the exhibition building and Armoury, its curved
facade developing into a glass stair tower as an eye-
catcher.

With 4,700 m² of floor space overall, at first basement
level the building takes up the entire plot for the main
exhibition area. In the three storeys above this there are
further presentation rooms of varying sizes and heights,
so that up to four different exhibition themes can be dis-
played on a total area of ca. 2,600 m². A small auditorium with 57 seats, a museum shop, several small
workshop rooms and a complete second basement level
as an interim depository and technical area complete the
internal arrangement.

That the model shown in January 1997 and the com-
puter simulation presented on the occasion of the first sod
being turned on 27 August 1998 did not promise more

8

9   10

„Sehen und gesehen werden". Durch die vordere Glasfassade sind die inneren Bewegungen wie durch ein Schaufenster zu verfolgen. Gleichzeitig wird dem Museumsbesucher die bisher vernachlässigte Nordfassade des Zeughauses durch die Glashalle wie in einem Rahmen gefasst präsentiert. Der angeschlossene gläserne Treppenturm, am Abend ein leuchtender Anziehungspunkt, ist der einzige Bereich, der sich hinter der gewaltigen Masse des barocken Zeughauses herauslöst und der bereits von der Straße Unter den Linden aus zu erkennen ist. Die Wendeltreppe des Turmes ragt aus dem Volumen der Glashalle heraus und inszeniert zwischen Innen- und Außenraum eine bewusste Präsentation des historischen Umfeldes. I.M. Pei hat mit dieser Blickachse zum Zeughaus und zum Forum Fridericianum eine architektonische Korrespondenz zwischen den Bauwerken der Vergangenheit und der Gegenwart geschaffen.

Das Volumen der Glashalle fordert den Besucher in nahezu piranesischem Sinne auf, das Museum mit seinen unterschiedlichen Raumbezügen und vertikalen Erschließungsmöglichkeiten aus immer neuen Perspektiven zu erkunden. Vom Verbindungsgang, der aus dem Schlüterhof kommend bereits erdgeschossig den Durchblick zum Neubau ermöglicht, öffnet sich im Untergeschoss ein großer Freiraum, der den ungestörten Blick bis in den Himmel freigibt. Diese atemberaubende Großzügigkeit hat ihren Ursprung in den eng gesteckten denkmalpflegerischen Vorgaben, die Pei auf elegante Weise berücksichtigt hat. Von den Rolltreppen, Freitreppen, Brücken und Galerien aus fällt der Blick immer wieder auf die gegenüberliegende Fassade des Zeughauses. „Urban theatre" – so bezeichnete Pei selbst seinen Museumsbau, von dessen verschiedenen Ebenen sich beeindruckende Perspektiven in den städtischen Raum eröffnen.

than they could deliver, professionals and the general public alike were able to judge for themselves four years later at the topping-out ceremony on 16 April 2002.

Transparency, movement and light are the means Pei uses to make the building into a public place – 'seeing and being seen'. Movement inside the building is visible through the glass front, as in a picture window. At the same time, the visitor inside the Museum gets to see the hitherto neglected north front of the Armoury, framed by the glass hall. The adjacent glass stair tower, a beacon of attraction after dark, is the only feature to stand out behind the huge mass of the Baroque Armoury so it can be seen from Unter den Linden. The spiral staircase of the tower rises out of the volume of the glass hall, and from it you necessarily become aware of the historic setting. With this perspective on the Armoury and the Forum Fridericianum, Pei has established an architectural correspondence between the buildings of past and present.

The volume of the glass hall prompts the visitor in an almost Piranesian fashion to explore the museum from different viewpoints and discover its various spatial relationships and vertical vistas. Coming from the Schlüterhof in the old building via the connecting passage, whence you can see into the new building even at ground floor level, a large airy space beginning at basement level opens up through the building, letting in the sunlight. This breathtaking free-handedness goes back to the closely specified conservation requirements, which Pei thus takes elegantly into account. From the escalators, steps, walkways and galleries you are constantly offered views of the facade of the Armoury opposite. 'Urban theatre' is what Pei himself called his museum building,

11   12   13

Die Ausstellungsräume liegen in einem mit Naturstein verkleideten, weitgehend geschlossenen Baukörper. Sie sind aus konservatorischen Gründen überwiegend fensterlos, der Bezug zur Grundgeometrie, dem Dreieck, bleibt jedoch überall erhalten. Lediglich im 2. Obergeschoss gibt es auf Wunsch von Pei Einschnitte in den monolithischen Körper: Ein gebogenes Fenster fokussiert die Neue Wache mit dem umgebenden Kastanienwäldchen; eine Dachterrasse und ein gläserner Erker schaffen den Blickbezug zur Museumsinsel.

Dieser, auch durch die Verwendung von Naturstein sehr skulptural wirkende und mit seinen zahlreichen Überschneidungen, Vor- und Rücksprüngen terrassenartig ausgebildete Baukörper wird von der über vier Geschosse reichenden offenen Glashalle umgriffen. Auf der Ostseite, unmittelbar an das Verwaltungsgebäude des Deutschen Historischen Museums angrenzend, ist ein schmaler, L-förmiger Baukörper eingestellt, in dem sich das Auditorium und Restaurierungswerkstätten befinden. Auch hier begrenzen die der Grundgeometrie folgenden Wände reliefartig die Glashalle.

Mit seinen Materialien passt sich das Gebäude den gegenüberliegenden klassizistischen Bauten an und setzt doch zugleich ein Zeichen der zeitgenössischen Moderne.

Die Außenfassaden der geschlossenen Baukörper sowie die Wände in der Glashalle sind mit einer Natursteinverkleidung aus fein geschliffenem französischem Kalkstein („Magny Le Louvre") mit geschlossener Verfugung versehen. Die tragenden Geschossdecken wurden aus so genanntem „Architekturbeton", einem speziell eingefärbten Beton gefertigt, dessen Struktur durch eine fein gemaserte Holzverschalung aus „Oregon Pine" herausgearbeitet wurde. Der an der Oberfläche geflammte nordamerikanische Granit

where you get impressive views of the urban environment at different levels.

The exhibition rooms are in a largely enclosed section clad in stone. For conservation reasons they are largely windowless, but the relationship with the basic geometry of the triangle is preserved everywhere. Only in the second storey were, at Pei's insistence, openings inserted into the monolithic exterior. An arched window looks out towards the Neue Wache and surrounding woods, while a roof terrace and glazed oriel offer a view of Museum Island.

The use of stone gives the building a very sculptural feel, but with its numerous intersections, projections and recesses, the terrace-like structure is surrounded by a four-storey open glass hall. On the east side, directly adjacent to the administrative building of the German Historical Museum, is a narrow, L-shaped block where the auditorium and restoration workshops are housed. Here too the walls follow the basic geometry and demarcate the glass hall like a relief.

With its materials, the building fits in well with Schinkel's Neoclassical buildings opposite but is at the same time a symbol of contemporary modernism.

The external facades of the enclosed building and walls in the glass hall are clad in a highly polished French limestone called Magny le Louvre fitted flush. The load-bearing ceilings were made of 'architectural concrete', a specially coloured concrete whose struc-ture was shaped by a fine-grained wooden framework of Oregon pine. The floors of both the exhibition building and the Schlüterhof are covered with waved North American Mason granite speckled beige and pink, the use of identical materials providing

14

„Mason" mit beige- und rosafarbenen Einsprenkelungen bedeckt die Böden des Ausstellungsbaues sowie des Schlüterhofes und verbindet beide Gebäude auch durch das gewählte Material miteinander. Glasfassade und Brüstungen wurden aus eisenoxidarmem und daher besonders weißem Glas hergestellt.

In den Ausstellungsbereichen wurde auf eine flexible Versorgungstechnik geachtet: Die Böden sind als Doppel-böden ausgeführt, in denen die gesamte Lüftungs- und Elektrotechnik geführt wird. Die quadratischen Boden-platten, deren Oberfläche aus Eichenparkett besteht, können gegen Platten mit Elektroauslässen ausgewechselt werden, so dass die Stromversorgung an jeder beliebigen Stelle des Raumes gewährleistet ist.

Beleuchtet wird das Gebäude durch Downlights. Die Akzentbeleuchtung in den Ausstellungsräumen erfolgt über Lichtschienen, die dem Dreiecksraster des Gesamtkonzeptes folgen. Lediglich im 2. OG sind diese Dreiecke als Tetraeder ausgebildet, um die Decke des höchsten Raumes durch eine zusätzliche Dreidimensionalität zu akzentuieren.

Besucher können den Neubau von der Straße Unter den Linden und von der Museumsinsel aus durch einen eigenen, an den Treppenturm anschließenden Haupteingang betreten. Ebenso können sie aber den Weg durch das Zeughaus neh-men. Man überquert den nach einem Entwurf von I.M. Pei mit Glas überdachten Innenhof, den Schlüterhof, und gelangt durch den ins Zeughaus eingeschnittenen, hoch überwölbten Verbindungsgang im Nordflügel über eine Rolltreppe in die große, lichtdurchflutete Glashalle. Dieser Einschnitt hat zur Folge, dass der Rundgang durch die Dauerausstellung nicht unterbrochen werden muss, und zudem ermöglicht er es, unter Terrain zu kommen, da das

another link between the two buildings. The glass facade and balustrades were made of a glass with a low iron oxide content which is therefore particularly white.

In the exhibition areas, a very flexible maintenance sys-tem was provided – the floors are built as double floors containing all the ventilation and electricity technology. The square floor slabs, the surface of which is oak parquetry, can be swapped for slabs with electrical outlets, so that electricity can be supplied at any point.

The building is illuminated by downlights. Highlighting in the exhibition areas is effected by tracked lighting that continues the overall triangular theme. Only in the second storey do these triangles become tetrahedrons, to lend the ceiling of the highest room additional three-dimensionality.

Visitors can enter the new building from Unter den Linden and Museum Island via a main entrance next to the stair tower, or alternatively they can come through the Armoury. You cross the Schlüterhof, an inner courtyard glassed over to a design by Pei, pass through the high-vaulted connecting passage inserted through the Armoury in the north wing via an escalator and eventually reach the large, light-filled glass hall. The consequence of this inserted passage is that a tour of the permanent exhibi-tion does not have to be broken off. It also makes it pos-sible to get below ground, as the Armoury has no cellar. By roofing over the Schlüterhof an additional space was created that can be used all year round. Here Pei creates a link with the post-1880 state of the building, when the northern part of the Armoury was remodelled after the Franco-Prussian War to create a hall of fame.[9]

Pei always saw the Armoury courtyard as a meeting place that would be full of life. He imagined an interior

31

Zeughaus nicht unterkellert ist. Mit der Überdachung des Schlüterhofes entstand ein zusätzlicher, ganzjährig nutzbarer Raum, der die Museumsbesucher zum Verweilen einlädt. Pei knüpft hier an den Bauzustand nach 1880 an, als nach dem Deutsch-Französischen Krieg das Zeughaus im nördlichen Teil zu einer Ruhmeshalle umgestaltet wurde.[9]

Pei sah den Zeughaushof immer als einen Ort der Begegnung, der mit Leben gefüllt werden sollte. Er stellte sich einen mit Bäumen begrünten Innenhof vor, in dem die Studenten der nahe gelegenen Humboldt-Universität tagsüber ins Café gehen und abends Musik hören können. Seine Idee scheiterte jedoch an der Ablehnung der Denkmalpfleger, die den Hof mit den Masken der Sterbenden Krieger von Andreas Schlüter in seiner Gestaltung erhalten wollten, und so auch den Charakter des „Steinernen Berlins".

Pei hat für die Wechselbeziehung zwischen Neubau und Zeughaus den Begriff „hand-in-glove-reciprocity" gefunden. Die funktionale und gestalterische Raumverbindung zwischen dem barocken Schlüterhof und dem modernen Erweiterungsbau bietet in der Tat zahlreiche verlockende Nutzungsmöglichkeiten.

Bei der Realisierung des Entwurfes stellte I.M. Pei sehr hohe Ansprüche bezüglich der Qualität von Material, Verarbeitung und Ausführung. Diese ästhetische Kompromisslosigkeit des Architekten war für die Projektmitarbeiter, die Fachplaner, die Bauverwaltung und die ausführenden Baufirmen eine große Herausforderung. Aber gerade die Ausführungspräzision und die strenge Materialauswahl sind das Geheimnis von Peis Meisterwerken aus Glas und Stein.

Im Laufe des Entstehungsprozesses gab es immer wieder Hindernisse technischer, personeller oder politischer Art, die es zu überwinden galt; manchmal schien die Situation so verfahren und ausweglos zu sein, dass ein Scheitern des Projektes zu befürchten war.

Nur der beharrliche Einsatz aller Beteiligten führte zu dem großartigen Ergebnis, das am 28. Februar 2003 bei der Schlüsselübergabe bewundert werden konnte.

In einem Interview wurde Pei einmal gefragt, was für ihn der schönste Augenblick bei einem Projekt sei. Er antwortete: „Was ich am meisten genieße ist das sich Erinnern an den Prozess des Überwindens der Schwierigkeiten, an all die Probleme, denen ich gegenüber stand und an all die Hilfe, die ich von verschiedenen Menschen erhalten habe, besonders von meinen Projektmitarbeitern und Kunden".[10] Für Pei ist daher der intensive Dialog mit seinen Auftrag-

courtyard full of trees where students from the nearby Humboldt University could go to the café or listen to music in the evenings. His idea failed due to the lack of approval. They wanted to keep the courtyard with Schlüter's masks of dying warriors in its original design and preserve the character of 'stony Berlin'.

Pei came up with the term 'hand-in-glove reciprocity' to describe the mutual relationship between the new building and the Armoury. The spatial link in design and function between the Baroque Schlüterhof and the modern extension really does offer numerous seductive opportunities for use.

In carrying out his design, Pei was fastidious in the quality and finish of materials he used, and the way they were installed. The architect's uncompromisingly aesthetic approach was a great challenge for everyone involved on the project – planners, building authorities and contractors alike. Yet it is the precision of execution and strict selection of material that is the secret of Pei's masterpieces of glass and stone.

During the genesis of the building, obstacles of a technical, personal or political nature kept cropping up, and solutions had to be found. Sometimes the situation was so muddled and hopeless that it seemed the project might collapse. Only perseverance on all sides led to the great result, which was opened to public admiration on 28 February 2003 on the handover of the keys.

In an interview, Pei was once asked what the finest moment of a project was. He replied: 'What I most enjoy is recalling the process of overcoming the difficulties, all the problems I had to face, and all the help I got from various people, especially from project collaborators and my clients.'[10] For Pei, a close, ongoing dialogue with his clients is therefore very important and the key to the success of a building.

This close, personal relationship between architect and client usually finishes up as a friendship. In the course of a project, people almost become members of an extended family. Even after the projects are completed, Pei remains in close contact with his clients, and this link remains intact over the years. The same has happened in our Berlin project. In the joint struggle for the best possible result, a very cordial relationship developed with Pei and his office over the years.

gebern sehr wichtig und ausschlaggebend auch für das Gelingen eines Bauwerkes.

Diese enge, persönliche Zusammenarbeit mündet meist in eine sehr freundschaftliche Beziehung zwischen Architekt und Auftraggeber. Man wird im Laufe des Projektes gleichsam Mitglied einer Großfamilie. Auch nach Fertigstellung der Projekte pflegt I.M. Pei einen engen Kontakt zu seinen „clients", der selbst nach vielen Jahren nicht abreißt. Dies gilt auch für unser Berliner Projekt. Im gemeinsamen Ringen um das bestmögliche Ergebnis entstand in den vergangenen Jahren ein sehr herzliches Verhältnis zu I.M. Pei und seinem Büro.

Anmerkungen:

1   Nach intensiven Überlegungen, bei denen kurzfristig als mögliche Bauplätze des Museums auch das Gelände des Völkerkundemuseums (westlich des Martin-Gropius-Baus), das Areal des ehemaligen Anhalter Bahnhofs, das südlich des Bendlerblocks gelegene Grundstück an der Stauffenbergstraße und vor allem auch das Gebiet, auf dem einmal das Prinz-Albrecht-Palais lag, in Betracht gezogen wurden, brachte 1986 ein städtebaulicher Wettbewerb die Lösung. *Deutsches Historisches Museum. Ideen – Kontroversen – Perspektiven*, hrsg. von Christoph Stölzl, Berlin 1988, S. 669

2   Ebenda, S. 670

3   Gratulationsschreiben von Willy Brand an den Regierenden Bürgermeister von Berlin Walter Momper, 17.03.1989, Archiv der Staatskanzlei, Berlin

4   Schon damals waren diese Gebäude als Erweiterungsbauten für Ausstellungen geplant gewesen. Als aber Ende der fünfziger Jahre die Entscheidung fiel, dass die im Krieg erbeuteten Kunstschätze aus der Sowjetunion wieder zurückgebracht werden sollten, mussten die Gebäude noch während der Bauphase in Depot- und Werkstatthäuser umgewandelt werden.

5   Gero von Boehm, *Conversations with I.M. Pei*, München 2000, S. 36

6   Carter Wiseman, *I.M. Pei. A profile in American Architecture*, New York [2]2001, S. 44 ff.

7   *Berliner Zeitung*, 17.1.1997

8   *Frankfurter Allgemeine Zeitung*, 20.1.1997

9   Regina Müller, *Das Berliner Zeughaus. Die Baugeschichte*, Berlin 1994, S. 165 ff.

10   Boehm, wie Anm. 5, S. 57

Notes

1   After lengthy deliberations, during which the grounds of the Ethnological Museum (west of the Martin Gropius Building), the area of the former Anhalter railway station, the land south of the Bendlerblock in Stauffenbergstrasse and particularly the site of the former Prinz Albrecht Palais were also considered, the solution was found in a town-planning competition in 1986. *Deutsches Historisches Museum. Ideen – Kontroversen – Perspektiven*, Christoph Stölzl (Ed.), Berlin 1988. p. 669

2   Ibid., p. 670

3   Congratulatory letter sent by Willy Brand to the mayor Walter Momper, 17.03.1989. Archiv der Staatskanzlei, Berlin

4   Even then, the buildings were planned as extensions for exhibitions. But when the decision was taken in the late-1950s that the art treasures looted during the war should be brought back from the Soviet Union, even while building work was under way the buildings had to be transformed into depository and workshop premises.

5   Gero von Boehm, *Conversations with I.M. Pei*, Munich 2000, p. 36

6   Carter Wiseman, *I.M. Pei. A profile in American Architecture*, New York 2001, p. 44 ff.

7   *Berliner Zeitung*, 17.1.1997

8   *Frankfurter Allgemeine Zeitung*, 20.1.1997

9   Regina Müller, *Das Berliner Zeughaus. Die Baugeschichte*, Berlin 1994, p. 165 ff.

10   Gero von Boehm, op. cit., p. 57

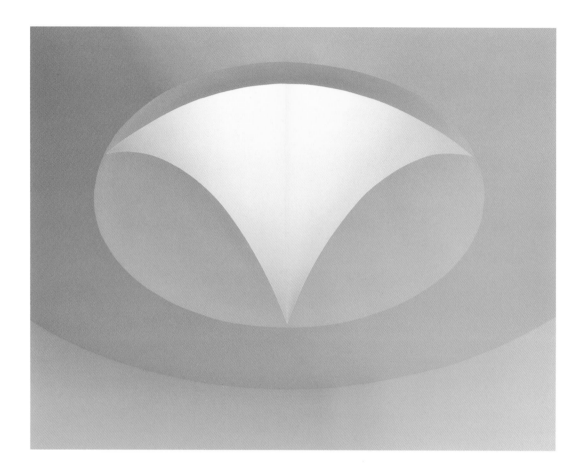

< Blick in einen Ausstellungsraum im zweiten Obergeschoss
View of a second-floor exhibition room

Oberlicht im Treppenhaus des zweiten Obergeschosses
Skylight in the stairwell of the second floor

Blick aus den Ausstellungsräumen im zweiten Obergeschoss
View from the second-floor exhibition rooms

Die Ausstellungsräume im ersten und zweiten Obergeschoss
The exhibition rooms on the first and second floors

Blick vom Werkstattbereich ins Foyer
View from the workshop area towards the lobby

Gebäudeschnitt durch das Zeughaus und das
Wechselausstellungsgebäude, Blick von Osten
Section through the Armoury and the Special
Exhibitions Building, view from the east

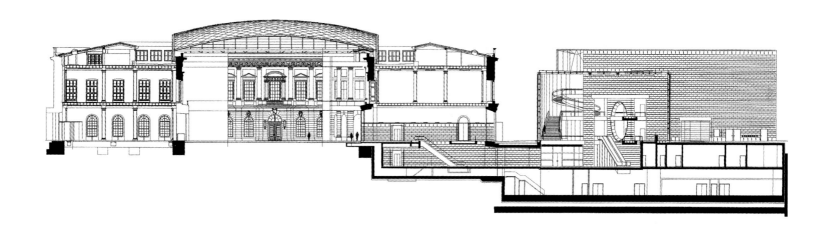

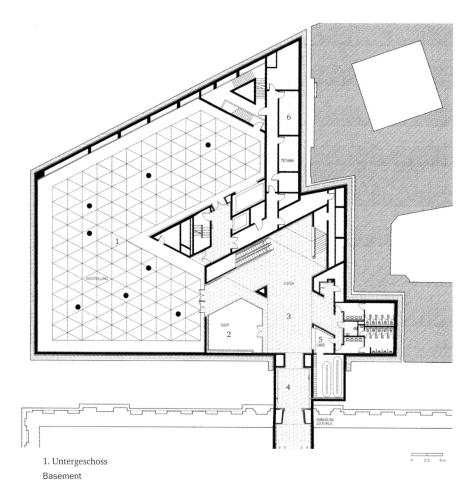

1. Untergeschoss
Basement

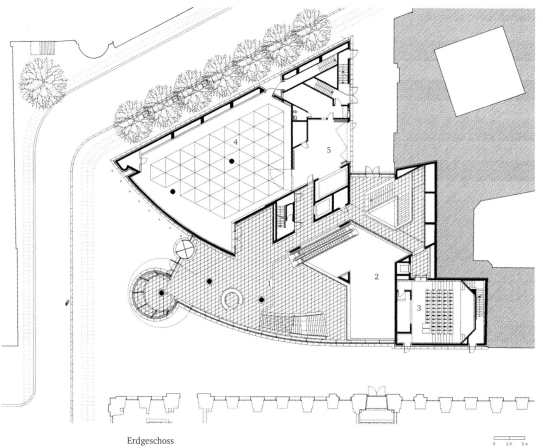

Erdgeschoss
Ground Floor

1. Untergeschoss
1 Ausstellungsbereich
2 Museumsshop
3 Unteres Foyer
4 Verbindungsgang/Passage zum
  Zeughaus
5 Garderobe
6 Technikbereich

Erdgeschoss
1 Foyer
2 Luftraum
3 Auditorium
4 Ausstellungsbereich
5 Anlieferung

Basement
1 Exhibition area
2 Museum store
3 Basement
4 Passage to Armoury
5 Cloak room
6 Technical area

Ground Floor
1 Foyer
2 Light well
3 Auditorium
4 Exhibition area
5 Delivery entrance

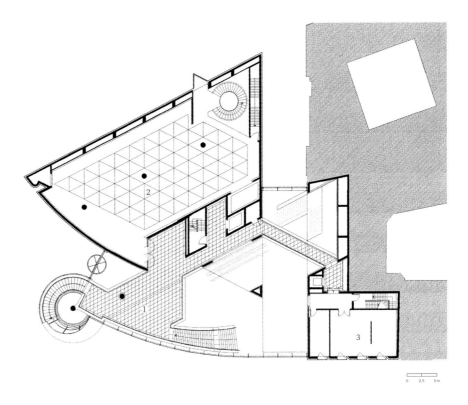

1. Obergeschoss
First Floor

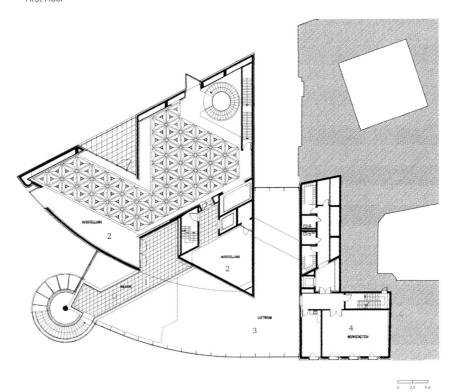

1. Obergeschoss
1 Balkon
2 Ausstellungsbereich
3 Werkstätten

2. Obergeschoss
1 Balkon
2 Ausstellungsbereiche
3 Luftraum
4 Werkstätten

First Floor
1 Balcony
2 Exhibition area
3 Workshops

Second Floor
1 Balcony
2 Exhibition area
3 Light well
4 Workshops

2. Obergeschoss
Second Floor

Bewegung und Transparenz
Movement and Transparency

Werner Sewing

Das Museum ist seit den siebziger Jahren des letzten Jahrhunderts zu einer der interessantesten Bauaufgaben für Architekten geworden. Wenn auch die Besucherzahlen in den letzten Jahren nicht mehr ganz so rasant zugenommen haben, so sind Museen doch zu einem öffentlichen Versammlungsort par excellence geworden. Sie besetzen zunehmend den Ort, an dem die Gesellschaft sich selbst begegnet, ihre Mitte sucht. Sie beerben oder profanisieren die sakrale und politische Feier des Gemeinschaftlichen, ohne allerdings deren verbindliche Kraft zu haben. Das Museum bietet vielmehr die einer individualisierten Gesellschaft angemessene Form der Begegnung und des gemeinsamen Erlebens.

Dieser Publikumserfolg des Museums ist durchaus zweischneidig, droht doch sein klassischer Bildungsauftrag in den Sog des Entertainment der Erlebnisgesellschaft zu geraten. Als öffentlicher Ort kann es nur solange gelten, wie es seine Inhalte nicht dem Zwang zur Vermarktung opfert. Auch die Museumsarchitektur gerät in Gefahr, sich selbst zum eigentlichen Kunstwerk zu stilisieren, so etwa das Guggenheim Museum von Frank O. Gehry in Bilbao. Andererseits: Warum

Since the 1970s, museums have become one of the most interesting commissions architects can go for. Even though visitor numbers have ceased to rise so exponentially in recent years, museums have nonetheless become prime venues for public congregation.

Increasingly, they are places where society likes to come together and seek its own heart. Museums have inherited or secularised the religious or political ceremonials of the community, though without acquiring the binding force of these. Museums are in fact a kind of meeting place and common experience that suits an individualised society.

Yet this success museums enjoy with the public cuts both ways. Their classic educational function is threatened by a sensation-based society's demand for entertainment. They can only remain public places as long as they do not sacrifice their contents to the compulsion of marketing. Museum architecture is likewise in danger of tricking itself out to become the real work of art, like Frank O. Gehry's Guggenheim Museum in Bilbao, for example. But then, why shouldn't good architecture constitute an attraction

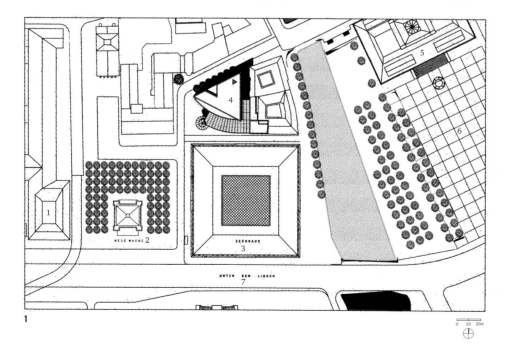

1

Lageplan
1 Humboldt-Universität
2 Neue Wache
3 Zeughaus
4 Neubau Wechselausstellungsgebäude
5 Altes Museum
6 Lustgarten
7 Unter den Linden

Site plan
1 Humboldt University
2 New Guardhouse
3 Armoury
4 Special Exhibitions Building
5 Old Museum
6 Formal gardens
7 Unter den Linden street

1 Lageplan des Erweiterungsbaus · Site plan of
the extension

2 Modell des Erweiterungsbaus im städtebaulichen
Umfeld · Model of the extension in its urban context

2

sollte gute Architektur nicht eine eigenständige Attraktion
sein? Gerade bei einem Museum mit wechselnden Inhalten
wird die Architektur von ihrem eher schlichten und neutra-
len Raumprogramm unabhängig und frei für die Feier, die
Inszenierung und Dramatisierung des öffentlichen Raums als
Selbstzweck. Öffentlicher Raum darf, nein: muss hier Luxus
sein, wenn die Atmosphäre des Außeralltäglichen des
gemeinschaftlichen Erlebnisses entstehen soll.
Museumsarchitektur ist gebaute Verführung. So unbestritten
die Qualität der Ausstellungen den Rang eines Museums
ausmacht, so wesentlich sind etwa die opulenten, häufig
kaskadenförmig gesteigerten Treppenhäuser, die Vestibüle
und Terrassen – die Räume, die das Museum erst zum Bewe-
gungsort einer festlichen, sensibilisierten Geselligkeit und
Öffentlichkeit werden lassen.

Bewegung und Transparenz, die „celebration of activity" –
mit diesen Begriffen umschreibt auch Ieoh Ming Pei seine
Entwurfsziele. Sie formulieren ein architektonisches Programm, dass den gebauten Raum als festliche, dramatische
Hülle und Bewegungsform begreift, nicht aber als Sensa-
tionskulisse. Wie kein Zweiter hat der inzwischen sechs-
undachtzigjährige Altmeister der amerikanischen Nach-
kriegsmoderne mit dieser Entwurfshaltung unser heutiges
Verständnis des Museums und damit den anhaltenden
Museumsboom befördert. Dabei hat er immer das Gleich-
gewicht zwischen Attraktivität und Gediegenheit, Sinnlich-
keit und Reduktion der Form gewahrt. Der Künstlerarchitekt,
dessen Bauherren häufig der Hochkultur verpflichtet waren,
geriet nie in die Untiefen vordergründiger Eventkultur.

of its own? Particularly in the case of museums with
changing exhibits, the architecture can shake off the pressure to produce rather plain, neutral spatial schemes and
adopt a stagey, dramatic approach to public space as an
end in itself, as celebration. Public space can, indeed
must be luxurious here if an atmosphere of non-mundane
shared public experience is to be created. Museum architecture is seduction in stone and glass. Though the quality
of the exhibitions is without doubt what confers status on
a museum, opulent, often cascading grand staircases,
lobbies and terraces are what set the tone. They are the
parts of the museum that turn it into a crucible of festive,
attuned conviviality and public congregation.

Movement and transparency, a 'celebration of activity'
are the terms Ieoh Ming Pei uses to describe the object of
his designs. They formulate an architectural programme
that sees built space as a festive, dramatic shell and type
of movement rather than a stage backdrop for sensation.
With this approach, the 86-year-old maestro of post-war
American modernism has, more than any other architect,
contributed to our present view of 'museums' and thereby
to the sustained museum boom. But, throughout, he has
nevertheless managed to preserve a balance between
good looks and solidity, sensory appeal and formal minimalism. As an art-minded architect whose clients were
often standard-bearers of high culture, Pei never lapsed
into superficial event culture. Besides a large number of
small museums in the American provinces, it was the construction of the striking East Wing of the National Gallery

45

Neben einer Vielzahl kleinerer Museen in der amerikanischen Provinz haben vor allem der Bau des markanten Ostflügels der Nationalgalerie in Washington von 1968–1978 und die zunächst umstrittene, dann gefeierte bauliche Reorganisation des Louvre in Paris mit dem starken Bild der Glaspyramide über dem neuen unterirdischen Eingangsbereich von 1983–1993 Peis Ruf als Magier des Raumes begründet. Sowohl die Transparenz der Pyramide aus Glas und Stahl als auch die Monumentalität der massiven Steinwände in Washington sind dem konsequenten Modernisten Mittel zur Steigerung des Ausdrucks der Form und zur Intensivierung des Raumerlebens.

So gab es denn auch 1995 trotz der vom damaligen Bundeskanzler Helmut Kohl allein getroffenen, an Mitterand erinnernden Entscheidung, I. M. Pei mit dem Entwurf des Erweiterungsbaus des Deutschen Historischen Museums zu betrauen, wenig Kritik in der Öffentlichkeit. Umso größer war die Erwartung, er werde dem bis dahin kaum wahrgenommenen Ort im Schatten des Zeughauses, zwischen den Monumenten Karl Friedrich Schinkels und Andreas Schlüters, eine kongeniale und zugleich zukunftsweisende Gestalt geben.

Pei hat dieser Erwartung entsprochen, er definiert den Ort neu, er wertet ihn auf und macht ihn zu einem baulichen Höhepunkt auf dem Weg von Schinkel zu Schinkel – von der Neuen Wache zum Alten Museum. Obwohl durchaus mit Respekt für den Kontext, erfindet er eine neue, fast radikale städtebauliche Figur und setzt sich souverän über das eherne Berliner Diktat des historischen Stadtgrundrisses hinweg. Für Pei sind Tradition und Moderne kein Gegensatz. Genius Loci, der Geist des Ortes ist für ihn nicht an das sklavische Befolgen eines Kanons gebunden. An Stelle der historischen, rechtwinkligen Ecke hinter dem Zeughaus, an der die sehr schmale Straße Hinter dem Zeughaus die Straße Hinter dem Gießhaus kreuzt, setzt Pei eine elegant und spielerisch zurückschwingende Glasfassade, die vor einer sich ebenfalls zurückbiegenden höheren Steinfassade liegt, diese aber nicht völlig bedeckt.

Der so entstandene neue Vorplatz schafft Distanz zu den Ikonen dieses Ortes um die Neue Wache, macht den Museumsanbau zu einem eigenständigen Gebäude mit einer Schaufront, dem „schönsten Hintereingang Berlins", so ein Journalist. Die gediegen verarbeitete Steinfront stößt mit einer leicht manieristischen, textil anmutenden Steinrolle erst dort an die Kante der Straße Hinter dem Gießhaus, wo diese in Richtung der Brücke zur Museumsinsel abbiegt.

in Washington (1968–78) and the initially controversial but later greatly lauded architectural reorganisation of the Louvre in Paris, with its powerful image of the glass pyramid over the new subterranean entrance area (1983–89), that established Pei's reputation as a conjurer of space. Both the transparency of the glass and steel pyramid in Paris and the monumentality of the massive stone walls in Washington are to the rigorous modernist a means of enhancing the expressiveness of design and intensifying the spatial experience.

Thus, even though, as with Mitterrand at the Louvre, the 1995 decision to commission Pei to design the extension to the German Historical Museum was taken by Chancellor Helmut Kohl alone, there was little public criticism of the choice. In fact, all the greater was the expectation that Pei would put forward a sympathetic and at the same time forward-looking solution for the rather overlooked site in the shadow of the Armoury (Zeughaus), between great historic set-pieces by Karl Friedrich Schinkel and Andreas Schlüter.

Pei came up trumps. He redefined and improved the site, creating an architectural landmark on the route from one Schinkel to the next, i.e. the Neue Wache (New Guardhouse) to the Altes Museum (Old Museum). While retaining the greatest respect for the setting, he came up with a new, almost radical planning configuration that sailed masterfully over the iron dictate of Berlin's historic urban landscape. For Pei, tradition and modernism are not antitheses. The genius loci is not bound up with slavishly following a canon. In place of the historic rectangular junction behind the Armoury where the very narrow back alley Hinter dem Zeughaus crosses Hinter dem Giesshaus street, Pei introduces an elegant and playful swept-back glass facade, which stands forward of a likewise inward-curving, higher stone facade but does not hide it completely.

The small square thus arising in front distances the great icons of the location around the Neue Wache while making the museum extension into an independent building with a show front – the 'finest back entrance in Berlin', in a journalist's words. The solidly handled stone facade only projects to the edge of Hinter dem Giesshaus with a slightly mannerist, textured-looking stone roll where the street veers off towards the Museum Island bridge. Only at this turn in the street does the massive, largely windowless block of the exhibition building becomes recognisable,

Erst an dieser Straßenbiegung wird der massige, weitgehend fensterlose Baukörper des Ausstellungsgebäudes erkennbar, der, auf dreieckigem Grundriss errichtet, auf vier Etagen die Ausstellungsräume ebenso wie Treppen, Fahrstühle und Funktionsräume beherbergt. Im Süden schließt an die abgerundete Seite des Dreiecks die großzügige Erschließungshalle an, die alle drei Etagen und ein Untergeschoss in einen durch Treppen, Stege und übereinander geschobene Zwischendecken vielseitig verrätselten Lichtraum transformiert. Die angesichts des eher kleinen Grundstücks gigantisch anmutende Halle mit ihrer zurückschwingenden Glasfront und einem komplett verglasten Dach öffnet einen fast irrealen Raum zwischen den Räumen. Die Rückseite des Zeughauses, das Palais am Festungsgraben, das Kastanienwäldchen und im Hintergrund die ruhige Wand der Humboldt-Universität werden entrückt, zugleich aber als Kulisse in die neu entstandene Welt zurückgeholt. Hier wurde ein fast magischer Raum geschaffen, der auch die Wahrnehmung des historischen Umfelds verändert. Das Museum wandelt sich zum öffentlichen Schauraum, in dem sich Transparenz und Bewegung wechselseitig zu einer neuen Einheit steigern.

Pei inszeniert in der Halle den Zusammenstoß und die Durchdringung des steinernen Dreieckskörpers mit der Transparenz des Glases in einer Vielzahl von Details. Dabei stiftet die durchgängige Qualität des hellen Steins – „Magny Le Louvre" aus einem Steinbruch bei Dijon – gleichwohl eine ästhetische Harmonie. Diesem Ziel dient auch die Einfärbung der sichtbaren Betondecken in derselben Farbe, was manchem Architekturpuristen wohl zu weit gehen mag.

Pei zitiert viele Leitmotive seiner früheren Bauten, etwa die Spindeltreppe, die schwingende Glasfront oder den hier über zwei Etagen gehenden Kreis in der Wand. Peis Architektur ist ihr eigener Kosmos und ihr eigener Zitatenfundus, sie ist selbstreferentiell. Der Rückgriff auf monumentalisierte geometrische Primärformen, auch der gigantische Okulus, der Kreis, erinnern an den 1974 verstorbenen amerikanischen Architekten Louis I. Kahn, den Pei noch kennen gelernt hatte und mit dem er die Vorliebe für freie geometrische Volumina teilt. Eine fast klassizistisch proportionierte Stahl-Glas-Front über drei Geschosse in der Mollergasse erinnert an den Klassizisten unter den Pionieren der Moderne, Mies van der Rohe, dessen Neue Nationalgalerie gerne mit Schinkels Altem Museum verglichen wird. Wenn man so will, ist dies auch der einzige Bezug auf Schinkel.

constructed on a triangular ground plan and accommodating exhibition areas on four floors together with staircases, lifts and functional rooms. In the south, the rounded side of the triangle adjoins the capacious entrance hall, which transforms all three floors and a basement into a light-flooded maze of staircases, walkways and stacked half-floors. The hall looks huge for the plot it occupies, and with its swept-back glass front and completely glazed roof opens up an almost unreal space between the rooms. The rear face of the Armoury, the Palais am Festungsgraben, the wood of chestnut trees and in the background the calm wall of the Humboldt University are set at a distance but at the same time exploited as stage sets in a newly created world. It is an almost magical space that has been created, one that also changes our perception of the historic environment. The museum is transformed into a public showroom in which transparency and movement reciprocally interact into a new, higher unity.

Pei's design for the hall incorporates numerous details highlighting the dramatic contrast and interpenetration of solid stone and transparent glass, but the consistent quality of the light-coloured stone – Magny Le Louvre from a quarry near Dijon – nevertheless provides an overall harmony. The exposed concrete ceilings in the same tones add to the harmony, though it may be a step too far for many architectural purists.

Pei introduces many motifs from his earlier works such as the corkscrew staircase, the sweeping glass front or the circle in the wall that here embraces two floors. Pei's architecture is its own cosmos and storehouse of quotations – in a word, self-referential. The resort to monumentalised geometrical primary shapes, and also the gigantic oculus, the circle, recall American architect Louis I. Kahn, who died in 1974. Pei knew Kahn personally and shared his preference for free geometric volumes. An almost classically proportioned, three-storey steel-and-glass front in Mollergasse is reminiscent of the neoclassicist among the pioneers of modernism, Mies van der Rohe, whose Neue Nationalgalerie is frequently compared with Schinkel's Altes Museum. If you like, this is also the only connection with Schinkel.

The triangle motif as a ground plan for an exhibition building, which arose quite as a matter of course from the site at the National Gallery in Washington, is entirely a conscious design choice in Berlin. There was quite enough room for a cuboid exhibition building. Once introduced, the

3

48

Das Motiv des Dreiecks als Grundrissform des Ausstellungsgebäudes, das sich bei der Nationalgalerie in Washington noch aus dem Grundstück zwanglos ergeben hatte, wird in Berlin nur formal begründet. Für einen rein kubischen Ausstellungsbau wäre durchaus Raum gewesen. Als formales Motiv dient das Dreieck denn auch in vielen Details, so auch als Musterung der Deckenstruktur. Ein Lastenaufzug ist als Folge dieser Grundrissform rautenförmig.

Dagegen steht östlich der Mollergasse ein weiteres eigenständiges Gebäude, ein sehr puristisch gestalteter, kubischer Baukörper mit perfekt proportionierten Fenstern, ein Muster minimalistischen Designs – poetischer Rationalismus pur, der an die Virtuosität der mediterranen Moderne erinnert. Der Bau, an den östlich ein schöner wilhelminischer Verwaltungsbau anschließt, – hier ist die Museumsleitung standesgemäß untergebracht – dient als Werkstattgebäude. Er ist über Betonstege im Erd- und ersten Obergeschoss über die hier zum Teil der Glashalle gewordene Mollergasse mit dem Ausstellungsgebäude und dem Foyer verbunden. Obwohl die Öffentlichkeit keinen Zutritt hat, möge sie versuchen, sich ihn zu verschaffen: Von hier bietet sich eine faszinierende Blickperspektive durch das Foyer. An der Mollergasse öffnet sich die Glashalle großzügig zum Untergeschoss, das mit einer Rolltreppe an das Straßenniveau angebunden ist. In Verlängerung der Mollergasse befindet sich unter der Straße Hinter dem Zeughaus, die nicht überbaut werden durfte, ein neu geschaffener unterirdischer Gang, der das Hauptgebäude des Museums, das Zeughaus, mit dem Ergänzungsbau verbindet. Der Aufstieg aus dieser „Unterwelt" in die Glashalle, unter den Stegen und aus der Untersicht konfrontiert mit dem monumentalen Okulus in der massigen, spitz zulaufenden Wand des Dreieckskörpers,

triangle also served as a formal motif for many details, for example the patterning of the ceiling structure. A goods lift is also diamond-shaped in response to this ground plan.

East of Mollergasse is a separate but contrasting building, a very purist, cuboid block with perfectly proportioned windows, a model of minimalist design – sheer poetic rationalism recalling the virtuosity of Mediterranean modernism. Adjoining a fine Wilhelminian administrative building on the east side – the Museum's administration is housed here as befits its station – this building serves as a workshop. It is linked with the exhibition building and the vestibule on the ground and first floors via concrete walkways across Mollergasse, which here becomes part of the glass hall. Although not open to the public, it is worth a visit if possible, because from here you get a fascinating view through the vestibule on the ground and first floor. On the Mollergasse side, the glass hall opens to the basement via a wide escalator opening which links the lower floor with the street level. Under the continuation of Mollergasse, i.e. Hinter dem Zeughaus, which could not be built over, is a new subterranean passage to the main building of the Museum, the Armoury, linking it with the extension. As you come out of this 'underworld' into the glass hall under the walkways, you are confronted with the monumental oculus seen in bottom view in the massive, sharp-edged wall of the triangular block. This constitutes yet another dimension of the spatial setting. The almost religious pathos of the sublime you experience as you come up into the light (it reminded one critic of a Piranesi flooded with light) might almost be considered over-dramatisation when set against the contents of the Museum.

The virtuoso orchestration of all the arts of visual surprise and the choreography of the hall as a constant enhancement of perception have created a work of art that is ultimately accessible only to a poetic sensibility. In a narrow sense, this is not functional space. The surface area even exceeds that of the functional rooms. In museum architecture, the architecture itself is also an exhibit.

ermöglicht noch einmal eine Steigerung der Rauminszenierung. Das fast sakrale Pathos des Erhabenen im Aufsteigen zum Licht, das einen Kritiker an einen mit Licht gefluteten Piranesi erinnerte, ist dabei, gemessen am Inhalt des Museums, fast zuviel der Dramatisierung.

Die virtuose Orchestrierung aller visuellen Überraschungskünste, die Choreographie des Raumes als ständige Steigerung der Wahrnehmung hat ein Gesamtkunstwerk geschaffen, das sich letztlich nur einer poetischen Sensibilität erschließt. In einem engen Sinne funktional ist dieser Raum nicht, in der Fläche übertrifft er sogar die Nutzräume: In der Museumsarchitektur ist auch die Architektur selbst immer Teil der Ausstellung.

Nicht nur im Foyer, auch aus den weitgehend geschlossenen Ausstellungsräumen erschließt der Architekt szenische Ausblicke nach draußen, so in einem dreieckigen Erker in den zwei Obergeschossen, der die Museumsinsel jenseits der Brücke zum Bild werden lässt.

Aber auch in die geschwungene Südseite ist an der Ecke der Schauseite über dem von der Steinrolle eingefassten vertikalen Schlitz ein perfekt justiertes Panoramafenster bündig im obersten Ausstellungsgeschoss eingelassen. Von hier bietet sich dem Betrachter ein wie komponiert wirkender Bildausschnitt, der alle baulichen Wahrzeichen der Umgebung, von der Neuen Wache bis zu den Kuppeln der St. Hedwigs-Kathedrale und einen der beiden Dome auf dem Gendarmenmarkt, verbindet. Pei arbeitet mit der suggestiven Bündelung und Bindung der Blicke der Besucher, er lenkt nicht nur die Wahrnehmung des Baus von außen, auch die Umgebung wird aus der Sicht des Innenraums zur kunstvoll stilisierten Vedute: Architektur als Augenlust.

Es ist nun gerade diese Schauseite des Erweiterungsbaus, die einigen Kritikern als Affront gegen die räumlichen Qualitäten dieses historisch wohl bedeutsamsten städtischen Raumes Berlins erscheint, den auch Pei für das „kulturelle Herz" der Stadt hält. Verlassen wir also das Innere und fragen nach dem städtebaulichen Kontext des Baus. Peis markante eigenständige Intervention verändert das Raumgefüge und führt eine andere Ästhetik ein, die historische Konventionen, etwa die axiale Anordnung stehender Fenster, ignoriert. Auch die forcierte Verwendung von Glas und dunklem Stahl in der geschwungenen Front der Treppenhalle, auch wenn hier fast klassische Proportionen gewahrt werden, ist in ihrer betont modernistischen Materialität ein Kontrapunkt zur umliegenden Steinarchitektur. Eine Provokation?

Not only in the foyer, but also in the largely closed exhibition rooms the architect opens up scenic views on surrounding areas, for example from a triangular bay window in the two above-ground storeys that look out on Museum Island beyond the bridge.

In the curved south front as well, at the corner of the facade there is a perfectly positioned panorama window inserted flush into the top exhibition storey above the vertical slit framed in the stone roll. From inside, this offers an almost composed pictorial scene that takes in all the built icons in the neighbourhood, from the Neue Wache to the domes of St Hedwig's Cathedral and one of the two cathedrals on the Gendarmenmarkt. Pei selects and combines views suggestively into artistically designed *vedute*, guiding the viewer's vision not only in the way the building is seen externally but also in internal views on the outside world. This is architecture to delight the eye.

It is this show front of the extension building that some critics see as an affront to the spatial qualities of this historically important part of urban Berlin, which Pei likewise considers the 'cultural heart' of the city. Let us therefore leave the interior and look at the urban architectural context of the building. Pei's distinctive, original intervention changes the spatial structure and introduces a different aesthetic that ignores historic conventions, for example the axial arrangement of standing windows. Likewise the forced use of glass and dark steel in the curved front of the stair hall, even if almost classical proportions are maintained here, acts in its emphatic modernist materiality as counterpoint to the surrounding stone architecture. Is this provocation, therefore?

When you consider the importance of this area in the history of state and city or conjure up its solid architectural air combining Neoclassicism and Baroque, the question arises as to Pei's historical self-positioning between tradition and modernism.

But perhaps we may first pursue the complexion of the historic location, perhaps the most important survival of the old royal and imperial city.

As the warm, soft yellow tones of Eduard Gaertner's paintings of the mid-nineteenth century suggest in a Romantic, almost Biedermeier style, the important public buildings of the Prussian state were concentrated within sight of the royal palace. The cultural and religious institutions of an Enlightenment period absolutist state

4   5

Bedenkt man die Bedeutung dieses Areals in der Geschichte von Staat und Stadt, beschwört man deren gediegene architektonische Aura zwischen Klassizismus und Barock, so drängt sich die Frage nach Peis historischer Selbstverortung zwischen Tradition und Moderne auf.

Zunächst aber sei der Aura dieses vielleicht wichtigsten historischen Gedächtnisorts der alten Residenzstadt nachgegangen. Wie es die in warmen, weichen Gelbtönen gehaltenen Gemälde Eduard Gaertners aus der Mitte des 19. Jahrhunderts in romantischer, fast biedermeierlicher Manier nahelegen, konzentrieren sich die repräsentativen Bauten des preußischen Staates in Sichtweite des Schlosses. Die kulturellen und religiösen Institutionen des aufgeklärt-absolutistischen Staates versammeln sich um das Forum Fridericianum und den östlichen Abschnitt des Boulevards Unter den Linden von der Schlossbrücke bis zum zweigeschossigen Marstall, der auch die Akademie der Wissenschaften beherbergte und erst 1903–1914 der neobarocken Staatsbibliothek weichen musste.

Der Platz um Schinkels Neue Wache mit dem Zeughaus, dem wichtigsten Barockbau nach dem Schloss, ebenfalls von Andreas Schlüter in seine endgültige Form gebracht, hingegen zeigte stärker das martialische Gesicht Preußens. Neben dem Sitz des preußischen Finanzministers, dem heutigen Palais am Festungsgraben, das erst ab 1861 seine heutige spätklassizistische Gestalt erhielt, gehören westlich davon die Singakademie und die Universität, ursprünglich als Palais für den Bruder des Königs geplant, zu den kulturellen Institutionen. Letztere wurde noch 1870 von dem bekannten

are grouped around the Forum Fridericianum, the eastern section of the Unter den Linden boulevard from the Schlossbrücke bridge to the two-storey Marstall, which also housed the Academy of Sciences and was only removed for the Neo-Baroque State Library in 1903–14.

However, the square around Schinkel's Neue Wache manifested the martial face of Prussia more noticeably. It included both the Armoury, the second most important Baroque building, and the royal palace (Stadtschloss), in its final form likewise the work of Andreas Schlüter. Apart from the Prussian finance ministry, now the Palais am Festungsgraben, which acquired its present late Neoclassicist guise only after 1861, the cultural institutions west thereof include the Singing Academy and the University, originally planned as a palace for the king's brother. The university was described by the distinguished scientist Emil Du Bois-Raymond even in 1870 as the 'intellectual bodyguard of the Hohenzollerns'.

The final element contributing to the military aspect of the genius loci of this section of Prussia's 'Via Triumphalis' was the rather marginal spot at the rear behind the Armoury, where Pei's building now stands. This originally contained the foundry (Giesshaus), where cannons and howitzers were cast. A modest two-storey building from Frederick the Great's time, it was demolished in the mid-1870s and replaced by barracks. Though their hard facade was subordinated to the richly ornamented Armoury, they nevertheless reached up to the eaves of the latter and occupied the rectangle between Hinter dem

4 Eduard Gaertner, *Ansicht des Gießhauses Hinter dem Zeughaus*, um 1860 · Eduard Gaertner, *View of the Foundry behind the Armoury*, ca. 1860

5 Die Straße Hinter dem Gießhaus mit Blick zum Palais am Festungsgraben, Vorkriegsaufnahme · Hinter dem Giesshaus street with a view of the Palais am Festungsgraben, pre-War photograph

6 Zeughaus mit überdachtem Schlüterhof und Kuppel der Ruhmeshalle im Nordflügel, 1937 · Armoury with covered Schlüterhof court and dome of the Hall of Fame in the north wing, 1937

6

Naturwissenschaftler Emil Du Bois-Reymond als „das geistige Leibregiment der Hohenzollern" bezeichnet.

Zur militärischen Grundierung des Genius Loci dieses Abschnitts der „Via Triumphalis" Preußens trug schließlich auch der rückseitige, eher periphere Ort hinter dem Zeughaus bei, an dem heute I. M. Peis Neubau steht. Hier befand sich das Gießhaus, in dem Kanonen und Haubitzen gegossen wurden. Das bescheidene, zweistöckige Gebäude aus friderizianischer Zeit wurde in den Mitte der siebziger Jahre des 19. Jahrhunderts abgerissen und durch eine Kaserne ersetzt, deren harte Fassade sich zwar dem reich ornamentierten Zeughaus unterordnete, aber dessen Traufkante erreichte und nun blockartig das ungleichseitige Viereck zwischen der Straße Hinter dem Zeughaus, der Straße Hinter dem Gießhaus und der nördlich vom Zeughaus im rechten Winkel abzweigenden Mollergasse besetzte.

Nach Kriegszerstörung und späterer Rekonstruktion des Zeughauses, von dem wie bei den meisten Rekonstruktionen in diesem Areal nur noch die barocke Fassade erhalten werden konnte, entstanden an dieser Stelle erst in den sechziger Jahren formal sehr zurückhaltende Depotgebäude für das Museum für Deutsche Geschichte der DDR, welche die kubische Gestalt der Gießhauskaserne wieder aufnahmen, allerdings die schräge Fluchtlinie nach Norden zugunsten von zwei rechtwinklig angeordneten Vorsprüngen ersetzten. Erst Pei nimmt nun mit seinem Ausstellungsgebäude auf dreieckigem Grundriss hier die straßenbegleitende Blockwand wieder auf und fasst diese als monumentale, penibel gefugte Fassade aus Kalkstein, einzig gegliedert durch einen über

Zeughaus, Hinter dem Giesshaus and Mollergasse as it branched off at the right-hand corner, north of the Armoury.

After the devastation of war and later reconstruction of the Armoury (as with most reconstructions in this area, only its Baroque facade could be retained), nothing was built on this site until the 1960s. Even then, the result was only two very restrained storage buildings for East Germany's Museum of German History. They echoed the cubic design of the Giesshaus barracks, though replacing the diagonal perspective to the north in favour of two rectangularly arranged projections. It was left to Pei with his exhibition building on a triangular ground plan to resume the block wall following the line of the street. He has made a monumental, precisely arranged facade of limestone out of it, punctuated only by a triangular, wholly glazed bay window in a steel frame rising over two storeys and a similarly triangular terrace inserted into the upper floor. In this formal minimalism, which makes the forcefully outlined wall particularly effective, the formal analogies with the dramatically heightened corner situation of his museum extension in Washington become particularly striking.

The storage buildings from East German days were originally earmarked for special exhibitions, but proved unsafe and in any case unsuited to the new museum. They were demolished even though their restrained facades, designed by Johannes Pässler after long debate among conservationists, wholly conformed with the rules

51

7

7 Depot- und Werkstattgebäude des Museums für Deutsche Geschichte, Zustand 1997/98 · Depository and workshop building of the Musem for German History in 1997/98

8 Ehemaliges Depot- und Werkstattgebäude, 1995/96 · Former depository and workshop building of the onetime East German Museum for German History, 1995/95

9 Abriss des Depot- und Werkstattgebäudes, Frühjahr 1998 · Demolition of the depository and workshop building, spring 1998

10 Das Wechselausstellungsgebäude im Bau, April 2001 · The Special Exhibitions Building during construction, April 2001

52

zwei Geschosse gehenden dreieckigen, vollverglasten Erker in einem stählernen Rahmen und einer ebenfalls dreieckig eingeschnittenen Terrasse im obersten Geschoss. An dieser formal reduzierten und damit besonders kraftvoll konturierten Wand wird auch die formale Analogie zu der dramatisch zugespitzten Ecksituation seines Museumsanbaus in Washington besonders augenfällig.

Die Depotgebäude aus der DDR-Zeit, ursprünglich ebenfalls für Wechselausstellungen geplant, schienen für das neue Museum ungeeignet. Sie wurden abgerissen, obwohl ihre zurückhaltenden Fassaden, nach langen denkmalpflegerischen Debatten von Johannes Pässler entworfen, durchaus den im Neuen Berlin geltenden Regeln der kritischen Rekonstruktion und der neuen Einfachheit entsprachen.

I.M. Peis bauliche Geste negiert diese stadträumliche Kontinuität. Auch als kritische Rekonstruktion kann seine konsequente Neudefinition des Ortes nicht verstanden werden. Er nimmt Abschied von der Tradition. Allerdings musste nach Intervention der Denkmalpflege die im ersten Entwurf von 1997 auf 21 Meter geplante Höhe des steinernen Ausstellungsblocks in der Realisierung auf 18 Meter reduziert, die zweiläufig konzipierte gläserne Spindeltreppe vor der Ecke der Glashalle auf eine Umdrehung begrenzt werden. Die ursprüngliche Kraft der geometrischen Primärformen der Volumina wurde zugunsten einer stärkeren Harmonisierung mit dem Umfeld abgeschwächt. Gleichwohl gelingt es auch dieser reduzierten Form, als kraftvolle Geste die Raumhierarchie des Ortes zu verändern und das Gesamtkunstwerk eines idealen preußischen Ortes der Zukunft zu öffnen.

Dabei ist Pei als „Mandarin der Moderne" weit von jeder avantgardistischen Attitüde entfernt. Vielmehr öffnet er den

of critical reconstruction and new simplicity that have now become de rigueur in the new Berlin.

Pei's architecture negates this urban planning continuity. His systematic redefinition of the site cannot be seen as critical reconstruction, either. He parts ways with tradition. Admittedly, the conservation department stepped in to scale back the height from the planned 69 feet of his first design to the 59 feet as built and reduce the proposed double spiral of the corkscrew staircase in the corner of the glass hall to a single spiral. The original forcefulness of the primary geometric shapes of the volumes was toned down in favour of greater harmonisation with the surroundings. Nevertheless, even in this reduced form, the building is a forceful statement that succeeds in changing the spatial hierarchy of the place and opens it up artistically as an ideal Prussian place of the future.

This is not in the least to suggest that Pei as a 'mandarin of modernism' is in any way being avant-garde.

8

9

10

Ort einer neuen, dem modernen Museumsbild innewohnenden Wahrnehmung aus der Bewegung heraus, die ihre Sensibilität stärker aus dem barocken Raumgefühl und der organischen Architektur des 20. Jahrhunderts bezieht. Als Kenner des fränkischen Barock eines Balthasar Neumann, dessen schwungvolle, dynamische Raumauffassung etwa der Wallfahrtskirche Vierzehnheiligen beim Meyerson Symphony Center in Dallas 1981-1989 Pate gestanden hatte, und beeindruckt von dem dynamischen Bewegungsraum der Treppenlandschaft in Hans Scharouns Berliner Philharmonie hat Pei die untergründige Wahlverwandtschaft dieser Bewegungsarchitektur mit den Anforderungen und Bedürfnissen der modernen Erlebnisgesellschaft verstanden.

Er steht damit sehr wohl in einer Tradition. Wenn er auch konsequent auf historische Anleihen verzichtet, fühlt er sich einer barocken, dynamischen Raumphilosophie verpflichtet. Wahrscheinlich hätte Karl Friedrich Schinkel, ansonsten ein scharfer Kritiker des historischen Barock, sich dieser neuen Synthese aus Moderne und barocker Sensibilität nicht verschlossen. Und auch die städtebauliche Konsequenz, mit der Pei, dessen große Projekte fast alle Solitäre waren, den Stadtraum öffnet und eine neue Platzform einfügt, steht der Raumvorstellung Schinkels, dem das historische Berlin keineswegs sakrosankt war, durchaus nahe. Zumindest in dieser Hinsicht war Schinkel Vorläufer einer architektonischen Moderne, wie sie I. M. Pei bei den deutschen Emigranten Walter Gropius und Marcel Breuer an der Harvard Universität kennen und an Mies van der Rohes Bauten in Chicago bewundern gelernt hat.

What he does is open the place up to a perception inherent in the modern movement-based concept of museums that draws its sensibility more strongly from a Baroque sense of space and twentieth century organic architecture. Being familiar with Balthasar Neumann's Franconian Baroque (e.g. the pilgrimage church of Vierzehnheiligen), whose sweeping, dynamic sense of space inspired the Meyerson Symphony Center in Dallas (1981– 89), and impressed by the dynamic movement space of the flight of stairs in Hans Scharoun's Berlin Philharmonia, Pei appreciated full well the underlying elective affinity of this architecture of movement with the demands and needs of our modern sensation-based society.

He thus does indeed continue a tradition. Even though he systematically dispenses with historical borrowings, he feels committed to a dynamic, Baroque philosophy of space. Probably Schinkel – otherwise a sharp critic of historical Baroque – would not have been averse to this new synthesis of modernism and Baroque sensibility. And the planning consistency with which Pei – an architect whose major projects are all unique gems – opens up this urban site and inserts a new type of square is altogether in line with Schinkel's concept of space. Historic Berlin was not sacrosanct even to Schinkel. In this respect at least he was a precursor of the architectural modernism that Pei learned to admire from Bauhaus emigrés Walter Gropius and Marcel Breuer at Harvard and Mies' buildings in Chicago.

Blick durch die Glasfassade ins Foyer
View through the glass facade into the foyer

Blick auf den Übergang zwischen Erweiterungsbau
und Zeughaus im Untergeschoss
View of the subterranean passage between the extension
and Armoury

Eingangsbereich im Untergeschoss
Basement-level entrance area

Verbindungsstege zwischen Werkstattbereich und Erweiterungsbau
Walkways linking the workshops and extension

Rolltreppen verbinden das Untergeschoss mit dem Erdgeschoss
Escalators link the basement with the ground floor

Treppe vom Foyerbereich im Untergeschoss zu den oberen Etagen
Stairs from the basement area to the upper floors

Abschluss des Handlaufs der Treppe zum Untergeschoss
Termination of the handrail on the stairs to the basement level

Eingangsbereich im Erdgeschoss
Ground floor entrance area

Blick vom Verbindungssteg zwischen Werkstattbereich und Erweiterungsbau ins Foyer
View of the lobby from the walkway linking the workshops and extension

Wandöffnung zwischen erstem und zweitem Obergeschoss
Aperture between the first and second floors

Aufgang vom Untergeschoss zu den oberen Ausstellungsräumen
The ascent from the basement to the upper exhibition rooms

Steinerner Handlauf an der Treppe zum Untergeschoss
Handrail of the staircase to the basement level

Blick durch die Wandöffnung im Erdgeschoss
View through the apertures on the ground floor

Eingangsbereich der Ausstellungsräume im ersten Obergeschoss
Entrance area to the first-floor exhibition rooms

Trägerelement der Dachkonstruktion
Girder in the roof structure

Glasfassade des Foyers mit Blick zum Zeughaus
Glass facade of the lobby with a view of the Armoury

Freischwingende Treppe zwischen
Eingangsbereich und erstem Obergeschoss im Foyer
Free-standing staircase from the entrance
area to the first floor in the lobby

Blick vom Eingangsbereich im Erdgeschoss zum Werkstattbereich
View from the entrance area on the ground floor into the workshop area

Ein Glasdach überspannt das Foyer
A glass roof covers the foyer

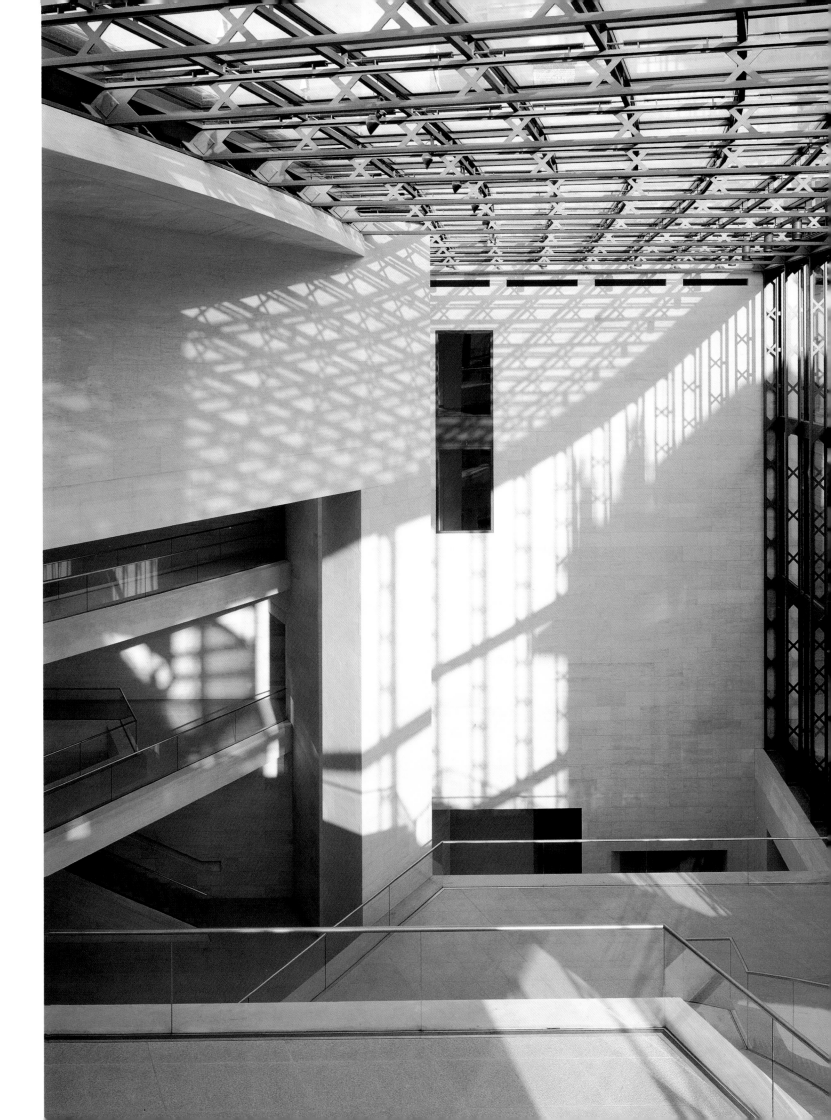

Übergang vom ersten Obergeschoss
zur gläsernen Spindel
Passage from the first floor to the glass
stairtower

> Blick aus dem gläsernen Treppenturm zum Palais
am Festungsgraben
View from the glass stairtower towards the Palais
am Festungsgraben

Runde Sitzbank im ebenerdigen Bereich der Spindel
Circular bench in the ground-level area of the glass tower

Blick aus dem Treppenturm zum Zeughaus
View of the rear facade of the Armoury from the glass tower

> Blick in das abendlich beleuchtete Foyer
Evening view of the illuminated lobby

Und ewig lockt der Raum
The Eternal Appeal of Space

Heinrich Wefing

In seinem langen Leben hat Ieoh Ming Pei beinahe alles gebaut, was ein Architekt bauen kann. Rathäuser und Konzertsäle, eine Kirche und einen Flughafen, ein paar Millionen Quadratmeter Bürofläche und sogar Sozialwohnungen. Aber in Erinnerung bleiben wird Pei seiner Museen wegen. Ein gutes Dutzend auf der ganzen Welt hat er errichtet, unter denen zwei hervorstechen: der East Wing der National Gallery in Washington, 1978 vollendet, und die grandiose Umgestaltung des Louvre, die sich von 1983 bis 1993 hinzog. Diese beiden Bauten haben Pei zuverlässig in die Sphären des Ruhms erhoben. Er selbst nennt das Museumsschloss in Paris das „wichtigste Projekt meines Lebens".[1] Es krönt eine Karriere, die sich beinahe so strahlend ausnimmt wie die nachts illuminierte Pyramide im Cour Napoleon des Louvre.

Museen zu bauen war eine Leidenschaft der vergangenen Jahrzehnte, in der sich Kunstsinn und Tourismusförderung, Bürgerstolz und Architektenego prächtig verbanden. Sie gipfelte Anfang der neunziger Jahre in einem wahren Rausch und brachte weltweit einige der spektakulärsten Bauwerke der Spätmoderne hervor: Richard Meiers Getty Center in Los Angeles, Frank O. Gehrys Guggenheim in Bilbao, Daniel Libeskinds Jüdisches Museum in Berlin, um nur die popularsten zu nennen. Natürlich hat auch Pei von dieser globalen Bauwut profitiert, aber die besondere Stellung von Museumsentwürfen in seinem Werk ist mehr als nur eine Konjunkturerscheinung. Sie hat mit dem Wesen seiner Architektur selbst zu tun. Seine Vorliebe für mächtige, äußerlich geschlossene Volumina entspricht zwanglos der Vorstellung vom Museum als kulturellem Speichermedium, als einer Institution also, die sich gegen die Zeit stemmt und deren Architektur daher durchaus eine gewisse Dauerhaftigkeit demonstrieren darf. Peis massige Kuben, anfangs, etwa beim Everson Museum of Art in Syracuse, New York (1964), noch in Sichtbeton ausgeführt, später in Sandstein oder Marmor verfeinert, signalisieren Beständigkeit. Gleich kostbaren Tresoren legen sie eine feste Hülle um die kulturelle Überlieferung. Peis Streben nach Perfektion, seine Sorgfalt im Detail, die Verwendung erlesener Materialien verleihen seinen Bauten zudem eine Anmutung des Zeitlosen.

In his long life, Ieoh Ming Pei has built almost everything an architect can build. Town halls and concert halls, a church and an airport, a few million square feet of office space and even council housing. But he will be remembered for his museums. Worldwide he has built at least a dozen, among them two that really stand out: the East Wing of the National Gallery in Washington completed in 1978, and the large-scale remodelling of the Louvre, which took from 1983 to 1993. These two buildings incontestably catapulted Pei into the realms of architectural fame. He himself calls the grand old museum in Paris 'the most important project of my life'.[1] It crowned a career that looks almost as brilliant as the pyramid in the Louvre's Cour Napoléon at night.

Building museums has been a universal passion in recent decades, when art-mindedness has come together with the promotion of tourism, and civic pride with architectural egos, with splendid results. It culminated in the early 1990s in a veritable effusion, creating some of the most spectacular buildings of Late Modernism all over the world – including Richard Meier's Getty Center in Los Angeles, Frank O. Gehry's Guggenheim in Bilbao and Daniel Libeskind's Jewish Museum in Berlin, to mention only the most popular. Of course, Pei himself also profited from this global building mania, but the special status of museum designs in his œuvre is more than just a phenomenon of boom times. It has to do with the nature of his architecture itself. His predilection for massive, externally closed volumes tallies perfectly with the

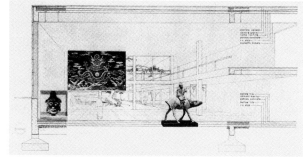

1

2

1 Entwurf für ein Museum der chinesischen Kunst in Shanghai, Abschlussarbeit an der Harvard Graduate School of Design, 1946 · Design for a museum of Chinese art in Shanghai, graduation project for Harvard Graduate School of Design, 1946

2 Everson Museum of Art, Syracuse, NY, 1961–64 · Everson Museum of Art, Syracuse, NY, 1961–64

3 Herbert F. Johnson Museum of Art, Cornell University, Ithaca, New York, 1968–73 · Herbert F. Johnson Museum of Art, Cornell University, Ithaca, New York, 1968–73

4 Rock and Roll Hall of Fame and Museum, Cleveland, Ohio, 1987–95 · Rock and Roll Hall of Fame and Museum, Cleveland, Ohio, 1987–95

Peis Architektur ist nicht für den Augenblick entworfen; sie soll bleiben. Vom Tag der Eröffnung an weht ein Hauch von Ewigkeit durch die Hallen, die seine Handschrift tragen.

Natürlich ist es nur ein biographischer Zufall, dass auch am Anfang von Peis Laufbahn ein Museum steht. Nach dem Grundstudium am Massachusetts Institute of Technology war der junge Mann 1942 nach Harvard an die Graduate School of Design gegangen, um bei den deutschen Emigranten Marcel Breuer und Walter Gropius seine Ausbildung zu vertiefen. Diese Lehrjahre haben Pei lebenslang geprägt, aber die liberale Atmosphäre der Schule erlaubte es ihm auch, in der Auseinandersetzung mit den Dogmen der ehemaligen Bauhäusler Ansätze einer eigenen Position zu entwickeln. Pei rieb sich vor allem an Gropius' Überzeugung, ein wahrhaft „Internationaler Stil" lasse sich überall auf der Welt einsetzen. Pei hingegen war überzeugt, der Architekt müsse die klimatischen, historischen und kulturellen Besonderheiten

idea of museums as cultural storage centres, i.e. institutions that stand firm against time and whose architecture is therefore certainly permitted to display a degree of permanence. Pei's solid cubes, initially built in exposed concrete (as for example at the Everson Museum of Art in Syracuse, New York, 1964) but later refined in sandstone or marble, demonstrate durability. Like expensive strong rooms, they lay a stout casing round cultural tradition. Moreover, Pei's striving for perfection, his attention to detail and use of fine materials lend his buildings a look of timelessness. Pei's architecture is not designed for the moment. It is meant to last. From the opening day on, a breath of eternity wafts through the halls that bear his signature.

It is of course only a biographical accident that Pei's career began with a museum as well. Following a foundation course at the Massachusetts Institute of Techno-

85

3

4

eines Ortes berücksichtigen, und um das zu beweisen, ersann er für seine Abschlussarbeit das Projekt eines Museums für chinesische Kunst in Shanghai, wo er vor seiner Übersiedlung nach Amerika gelebt hatte.

Am wichtigsten schien Pei die Eigentümlichkeit der Exponate. Werke der chinesischen Kunst, darauf bestand er, unterschieden sich fundamental von westlicher Malerei und Skulptur. Wichtige asiatische Gemälde zum Beispiel werden nicht an die Wand gehängt, sondern nur für kurze Zeit entrollt. Die klassische chinesische Kunst, erläuterte der junge Architekt in einem Aufsatz, sei zudem aus der Beobachtung der Natur entstanden, weshalb ihre Werke am besten in Blickweite eines Gartens ausgestellt würden.[2] Also schlug Pei für sein Museum of Chinese Art einen zweigeschossigen „Container" vor, der so um einen Teegarten herumgruppiert werden sollte, dass alle Ausstellungsbereiche eine Aussicht in den grünen Hof geboten hätten. Die Studie war trotz aller Bekenntnisse zur chinesischen Architekturgeschichte ersichtlich vom Bauhaus inspiriert. Sogar die Darstellungstechnik – eine perspektivische Zeichnung mit eincollagierten Kunstwerken – erinnert an die Vorbilder. Gropius notierte beeindruckt, das Projekt zeige, „dass ein fähiger Entwerfer an grundlegenden Traditionen festhalten kann, ohne eine progressive Konzeption des Entwurfs zu opfern."[3]

Unschwer lassen sich in der Studentenarbeit bereits einige der Motive ausmachen, die später Peis Werk prägen sollten. Die Auseinandersetzung mit der Vergangenheit beispielsweise, die Verschmelzung von Architektur und Natur, zudem Ansätze dessen, was man vielleicht als Peis deduktive Methode des Entwerfens bezeichnen könnte: seine Suche nach Lösungen, die sich aus der beharrlichen Analyse der Bauaufgabe ergeben. Noch deutlicher nimmt das Harvard-Projekt aber etwas anderes vorweg: Peis lebenslange Variation und Verfeinerung der klassischen Moderne. Das wesentliche Charakteristikum seiner Architektur, schreibt Peis Biograph Carter Wiseman, ist „die kreative Vervollkommnung" des Überlieferten.[4]

Man hat Pei einen „Vollender der Moderne" genannt. Tatsächlich wurzelt sein architektonisches Vokabular tief in den Traditionen des frühen 20. Jahrhunderts. Er steht zum Urgestein des Neuen Bauens wie die Klassizisten zu Bramante oder Palladio standen – er ist ein einfallsreicher, gelegentlich manieristischer Bewunderer ihrer Kunst, aber kein Kopist. Vorzugsweise arbeitet er mit klaren Volumina und simplen geometrischen Körpern aus Glas oder Stein, die er so kombiniert, dass sich aus dem Ineinander eine latente

86

logy, the young man moved on to the Graduate School of Design at Harvard in 1942, to continue his studies under German emigrants Marcel Breuer and Walter Gropius. These years left an indelible impression on Pei, but the school's liberal atmosphere also enabled him to develop a tentative voice of his own in his tussle with the doctrines of the former Bauhaus teachers. Pei particularly parted company with Gropius' conviction that a real 'international style' could be applied all over the world. Pei's view was that an architect should take the climate, history and cultural particularities of a place into account, and to demonstrate this he devised for his final thesis a project for a museum for Chinese art in Shanghai, where he had lived before he settled in America.

For Pei, the most important consideration in a museum was the singularity of the exhibits. Works of Chinese art, he insisted, were fundamentally different from western painting and sculpture. Important Asiatic paintings for example are not hung on the wall but only unrolled for a short time. Furthermore, classic Chinese art, explained the young architect in an essay, evolved from the observation of nature, so that its works were best exhibited in the context of a garden.[2] Pei therefore proposed for his Museum of Chinese Art a two-storey 'container' grouped round a tea garden in such a way that all exhibition areas would have a view into the green courtyard. Yet despite all the nods in the direction of Chinese architectural history, the study was visibly inspired by the Bauhaus. Even the depiction technique – a perspective drawing with artworks collaged in – is reminiscent of this source. Impressed, Gropius noted that the project showed that a competent designer could stick to basic traditions without sacrificing a progressive concept of design.[3]

It is not difficult to identify in this student thesis some of the themes that would feature in Pei's later work – the involvement with the past for example, the blending of architecture and nature, and also beginnings of what one might term Pei's deductive method, i.e. his search for solutions generated by an exhaustive analysis of the building task. But even more than this, the Harvard project anticipates something else – Pei's lifelong variation and refinement of classic modernism. The essential feature of his architecture, writes Pei's biographer Carter Wiseman, is 'the creative perfection' of the traditional.[4]

Pei has been called a 'consummator of modernism'. His architectural vocabulary is indeed deeply rooted in the

Spannung ergibt. In dem Wort von der „Vollendung" der Moderne schwingt allerdings auch eine Ahnung von Ende mit, und auch diese Lesart trifft zu. Der 1917 in China geborene, seit 1934 in den Vereinigten Staaten lebende Pei ist ein eleganter Konservativer, der seine Architektur zu einer Reife getrieben hat, die etwas Finales besitzt. Die Variationen seines Vokabulars bringen immer wieder Bauwerke hervor, die Nutzer und Besucher erfreuen, die aber kaum mehr überraschen. Das Werk ist erprobt, bewährt – und abgeschlossen. Wohin es sich noch entwickeln könnte, ist schwer zu erkennen. Und wagt Pei doch einmal, aus den Umklammerungen seiner Klassizität auszubrechen, dann ist er dem Scheitern recht nahe. Sein Versuch etwa, bei der Rock'n'Roll Hall of Fame in Cleveland etwas beschwingter und dekonstruktivistischer zu sein als üblich, vielleicht gar ein wenig frivol, ist gründlich missraten. In seiner angestrengten Verdrehtheit gleicht der Ruhmestempel des Rock einem Rentner in der Diskothek.

Für gewöhnlich jedoch weiß sich Peis Architektur den Erfordernissen einer Aufgabe anzuschmiegen. Wohl nicht zufällig sind viele seiner Museumsprojekte Anbauten oder Erweiterungen: der East Wing der Nationalgalerie in Washington, der West Wing des Museum of Fine Arts in Boston (1981), die Umgestaltung des Louvre und natürlich das Wechselausstellungsgebäude des DHM. Diese Bereitschaft zum Weiterbauen, das Denken in Zusammenhängen statt in Solitären ist vielleicht das wesentliche Merkmal, das Peis Arbeit von der Architektur anderer Großarchitekten unterscheidet. Mies stellte einst überall die gleichen Glaskisten ab, ohne sich um die Nachbarschaft zu scheren, und Frank O. Gehry lässt an jedem Ort der Erde wild zuckende Metallgewitter niedergehen. Pei hingegen nimmt Rücksicht – auf die Altbauten nebenan, auf die Erfordernisse des Quartiers, auf das Grün der Umgebung. So entstehen, trotz der Repetition bestimmter Motive, erstaunlich unterschiedliche Bauwerke.

Es gibt zum Beispiel den grazilen Brutalismus des Herbert F. Johnson Museum of Art in der Cornell University in Ithaca, New York (1973), ein Kubengeschiebe in Sichtbeton; es gibt den Wechselausstellungsbau des DHM, der mit der Präzision eines Uhrmachers in den Stadtraum hinter Schlüters Zeughaus eingepasst worden ist; es gibt die meditative Geometrie des Miho Museums in Japan (1997), das beinahe wie ein altersweises Echo von Peis Studentenentwurf eines Museums für chinesische Kunst erscheint. Das lang gestreckte Gebäude auf einem Bergrücken unweit von Kyoto beherbergt eine

traditions of the early twentieth century. He cleaves to the rock of 1927 Neues Bauen just as the Neoclassicists clung to Bramante or Palladio – he is an imaginative, occasionally mannerist admirer of the style but no copyist. For preference, he works with clear volumes and simple geometric bodies of glass or stone, which he brings together so as to create a latent tension in the combination. In the term 'perfection' of modernism there is of course an implied notion of ending as well, and this interpretation is also accurate. Born in China in 1917 but settled in the USA since 1935, Pei is an elegant conservative who has taken his architecture to a maturity that has a quality of finality. The variations of his vocabulary keep producing buildings that users and visitors enjoy but hardly surprise them any more. The œuvre is tried, tested – and concluded. Whether it could still develop is difficult to perceive. And when Pei ventures to break out of the confines of his classicism, he comes close to running aground. For example, his attempt to be somewhat more exuberant and deconstructivist than usual – perhaps even a little frivolous – in the Rock and Roll Hall of Fame in Cleveland was thoroughly misconceived. In its forced zaniness, the Hall of Fame is rather like a pensioner in a discotheque.

But ordinarily Pei's architecture is fully up to the challenge of a commission. It is probably no accident that many of his museum projects are annexes or extensions, e.g. the East Wing of the National Gallery in Washington, the West Wing of the Museum of Fine Arts in Boston (1981), the remodelling of the Louvre and of course the Schauhaus of the German Historical Museum. This readiness to extend, to think in given contexts instead of grand stand-alone set-pieces, is perhaps the most important characteristic that distinguishes Pei's work from the architecture of other great architects. Mies used to drop the same glass boxes everywhere without a thought for the setting, and Frank O. Gehry unleashes wildly thrashing storms of metal all over the world. Pei on the other hand shows consideration – for the old buildings alongside, for what the district needs, for the greenery in the area. So despite the repetition of certain motifs, astonishingly different buildings are the result.

There is for example the gracile brutalism of the Herbert F. Johnson Museum of Art at Cornell University in Ithaca, New York (1973), a scrum of cubes in exposed concrete; there is the special exhibitions building of the German Historical Museum, which has been inserted

erlesene Sammlung asiatischer Kunst. Es ist um Höfe und Gärten arrangiert, von dichter Vegetation eingefasst und bietet atemraubende Aussichten in die Bergwelt ringsum. Mit Rücksicht auf strenge Naturschutzgesetze musste Pei den Bau tief in den Berg eingraben. Von Ferne sind nur die Glasdächer zu erkennen. Sie lassen Tageslicht in die Ausstellungsbereiche einfallen und nehmen den versenkten Galerien alles Höhlenartige. Fast meint man, Pei habe all das demonstrieren wollen, was er fünfzig Jahre zuvor in seiner Abschlussarbeit gefordert hatte: Respekt vor den klimatischen und kulturellen Eigenheiten eines Ortes und mehr noch die Symbiose von Natur und Architektur.

Auch Peis Hauptwerke, der Louvre in Paris und der East Wing in Washington, sind sorgsam eingebettet in ihr historisches und urbanistisches Umfeld. Beide Bauten mögen längst zu Monumenten aus eigenem Recht geworden sein, doch lassen auch sie sich nur verstehen, wenn man sie als Fortschreibung des Bestehenden begreift.

Mit den Planungen für den Ostflügel der amerikanischen Nationalgalerie war bereits Mitte der fünfziger Jahre begonnen worden, als sich abzeichnete, dass der bestehende neoklassizistische Tempel bald nicht mehr ausreichen würde, die wachsenden Sammlungen sowie ein neues Studienzentrum für Kunstgeschichte aufzunehmen. Für die Erweiterung stand ein benachbartes Grundstück zur Verfügung, das zwar direkt an der Mall, der imperialen Prachtachse Washingtons, lag, jedoch sehr unglücklich geschnitten war. Der auserkorene Bauplatz schräg gegenüber des Kapitols war kaum mehr als eine Restfläche, die sich beim spitzwinkeligen Zusammentreffen zweier Avenuen ergeben hatte. Ehe Pei

5

into the urban space behind Schlüter's Armoury with a watchmaker's precision; there is the meditative geometry of the Miho Museum in Japan (1997), which looks almost like the mature Pei revisiting his student design for a museum of Chinese Art. The elongated building on a mountain ridge not far from Kyoto houses an exquisite collection of Asiatic art. It is arranged around courts and gardens, set in dense vegetation and offering breathtaking views towards the surrounding mountains. In deference to strict nature conservation laws, Pei had to sink the building deep into the mountain. From a distance, only the glass roofs are recognisable. They admit daylight into the exhibition areas and offset any cave-like propensities in the sunken galleries. One might almost think that Pei wanted to demonstrate everything that he advocated fifty years earlier in his student thesis – respect for the climate and cultural characteristics of a place, and even more the symbiosis of nature and architecture.

Even Pei's principal works, the Louvre in Paris and the East Wing in Washington, are carefully embedded in their historic and urban settings. Though both buildings have become monuments in their own right, even they can only be understood as a continuation of what was already there.

Work on planning for the East Wing dated back to the mid-1950s, when it became apparent that the existing Neoclassical temple would soon be inadequate to accommodate both the growing collections and a new centre for the history of art. A neighbouring plot of land was available for the extension. However, though this lay directly on the Mall, the grand imperial axis of Washington, it was nonetheless unfortunately situated. Diagonally opposite the Capitol, the earmarked site was scarcely more than a remnant produced by the junction of two avenues at an angle. Before Pei was given the commission, several architects had come to grief trying to come up with a convincing scheme for the thankless site. Moreover, despite all the unfavourable aspects, there were also the strict design conditions imposed by the local authorities to consider.

A number of rough sketches show how Pei solved the problems after being commissioned by the family of Museum founder Paul Mellon to do the planning. He came up with a configuration of two triangles, an isosceles triangle and an acute-angled triangle, which he so

6

den Auftrag erhielt, waren bereits mehrere Architekten mit dem Versuch gescheitert, für das undankbare Gelände ein überzeugendes Konzept zu liefern, und zu allen Widrigkeiten kamen auch noch strikte Gestaltungsauflagen der örtlichen Behörden hinzu.

Einige Handskizzen zeigen, wie Pei die Probleme löste, nachdem er 1968 von der Familie des Museumsstifters Paul Mellon mit den Planungen beauftragt worden war. Er ersann eine Konfiguration zweier Dreiecke, eines gleichschenkligen und eines spitzwinkeligen, die er so nebeneinander schob,

positioned next to each other that they fitted into the line of buildings as a matter of course and pick up every axis in the adjacent built environment. In the southern, sharp-ended slice is the Center for Advanced Study in the Visual Arts, while in the larger isosceles triangle are the exhibition rooms. The two buildings are linked by a like-wise house-height triangular hall crowned by a subtle glass roof. Once he caught on to the idea of the triangle as the basic element of the design, Pei developed solutions to all kinds of architectural problems from it,

5 Miho Museum, Shigaraki/Kyoto, Japan, 1991–97, Innenansicht ·
Miho Museum, Shigaraki, Kyoto, Japan, 1991–97, interior view

6 Das Museumsgebäude fügt sich perfekt in die hügelige Landschaft ein ·
The museum building fits into the hilly landscape perfectly

7

dass sie wie selbstverständlich in den Baufluchten liegen und alle Achsen der umgebenden Bebauung aufnehmen. In dem südlichen, messerscharf zulaufenden Tortenstück ist das „Center for Advanced Study in the Visual Arts" untergebracht, in dem größeren, gleichschenkligen befinden sich die Ausstellungssäle. Verbunden werden die beiden Baukörper von einer ebenfalls dreieckigen, haushohen Halle, über die sich ein raffiniertes Glasdach spannt. Einmal auf das Dreieck als das Grundmodul des Entwurfes verfallen, hat Pei daraus Lösungen für alle architektonischen Fragen entwickelt: Vom Fugenschnitt des Bodenbelags über das Design der Sitzbänke bis zum Betonraster der Decken – immer wieder taucht das Dreieck als zentrales Thema auf. So ist noch im kleinsten Detail der übergeordnete Gedanke präsent, und in jeder Winzigkeit spiegelt sich der Stadtgrundriss.

Äußerlich mutet Peis East Wing wie eine Skulptur an, die sich selbst genügt. Wer mag, kann den Ostflügel als isolierten Baukörper wahrnehmen, ohne der alten Nationalgalerie viel

ranging from the cut of the floor covering via the design of the bench seats to the concrete grid of the ceilings – the triangle reappears again and again as a central theme. The overarching concept is thus present in the smallest detail and the city plan is reflected in the minutiae.

Externally Pei's East Wing looks like a sculpture that is sufficient unto itself. Anyone so minded can see the East Wing as an isolated building, without taking much notice of the old National Gallery. Nevertheless, the two buildings, which are connected below ground by a foot tunnel, do not stand side by side like standoffish neighbours. New dimensions carefully attuned to the old, Pei's respect for the height of the old building and his use of the same building material – a gleaming pink marble from Tennessee – ensure harmony despite the contrasting styles. How well the sharp-edged sculptural building has been integrated into the sophisticated setting of the Mall is evident not least from the National Gallery's usual

8

9

Beachtung zu schenken. Gleichwohl stehen sich die beiden Bauten, die unterirdisch durch einen Fußgängertunnel verknüpft sind, nicht wie Fremdkörper gegenüber. Die sorgsam aufeinander abgestimmten Maße, Peis Rücksichtnahme auf die Höhenentwicklung des Altbaus, das einheitliche Material – hier wie dort ein rosa schimmernder Marmor aus Tennessee – sorgen bei aller formalen Gegensätzlichkeit für Harmonie. Wie gut die Integration der scharfkantigen Bauplastik in das mondäne Ensemble der Mall gelungen ist, lässt sich nicht zuletzt am internen Sprachgebrauch der Nationalgalerie erkennen. Statt von Hauptgebäude und Erweiterung reden Kuratoren und Direktoren nur vom Westflügel und vom Ostflügel wie von gleichberechtigten Teilen eines Ganzen.

name for it. Instead of talking of main building and extension, curators and directors only speak of west and east wings, as of equally important parts of a whole.

The East Wing undoubtedly helped Pei to secure the job of a lifetime. Impressed by the museum in Washington, French president François Mitterand discreetly asked the American architect in 1983 whether he might be interested in doing a makeover of the Louvre. Begun around 1190 and constantly rebuilt and added to since, the one-time royal residence and latterly grand cultural palace was in a lamentable condition at the time. Half of it was occupied by the French ministry of finance, the courtyards had become gloried car-parks, and apart from the art the exhibition areas displaying one of the best art

91

10

7   Ostflügel der National Gallery of Art, Washington, D.C., 1968–78 · East Wing of the National Gallery of Art, Washington, D.C., 1968–78

8   Im Atrium des Ostflügels · In the atrium of the East Wing

9   Blick auf das Capitol mit dem Gebäude der National Gallery und dem östlich gelegenen Erweiterungsbau · View towards the Capitol with the National Gallery building and its extension

10   Entwurfsskizze für den Erweiterungsbau · Design sketch for the extension

Der East Wing dürfte Pei auch zum Auftrag seines Lebens verholfen haben. Beeindruckt von dem Museum in Washington, erkundigte sich der französische Staatspräsident Mitterrand 1983 diskret bei dem amerikanischen Architekten, ob ihn die Umgestaltung des Louvre reizen könnte. Das ehemalige Königsschloss, begonnen um 1190 und immerfort umgebaut, befand sich damals in jammervollem Zustand. Die Hälfte des Palastes belegte das französische Finanzministerium, die Höfe waren zu Parkplätzen verkommen, und den Flügeln, in denen eine der besten Kunstsammlungen der Welt gezeigt wurde, fehlte abgesehen von der Kunst eigentlich alles, was ein bedeutendes Museum ausmacht: Ausstellungsflächen, Klima- und Sicherheitstechnik, Werkstätten, Restaurants und sogar Toiletten, vor

collections in the world lacked more or less everything that makes a major museum – adequate exhibition areas, air-conditioning and up-to-date security installations, workshops, restaurants and even toilets, and above all an attractive main entrance. Immediately on taking office, Mitterand decided to remedy all these, and launched an ambitious cultural programme for his presidency.

The ambitiousness of Pei's proposals were wholly to the taste of his client, but encountered furious protest from the public. When the architect first presented his scheme to the Commission des Monuments Historiques, he was attacked with such ferocity that his translator broke down in tears. After studying the wishes of users and examining the old building, Pei had come to the

11 Überglaster Innenhof im Grand Louvre, Paris, 1983–93
Glazed inner courtyard of the Grand Louvre, Paris, 1983–93

12 Freischwingende Rundtreppe vom Untergeschoss in die Eingangshalle der gläsernen Pyramide · Spiral staircase from the basement into the entrance area in the glass pyramid

13 Rolltreppen verbinden die einzelnen Ausstellungsebenen, großzügige Wandöffnungen lassen Tageslicht einströmen · Escalators link the various exhibition levels, while daylight is admitted via large wall apertures

14 Blick in den Cour Napoleon mit der Glaspyramide · View of the Cour Napoléon with the glass pyramid

allem aber ein attraktiver Haupteingang. Gleich nach seinem Amtsantritt beschloss Mitterrand, all diesen Übeln abzuhelfen und gab seiner Präsidentschaft damit ein ehrgeiziges kulturpolitisches Programm.

Peis Vorschläge waren in ihrer Ambition ganz nach dem Geschmack des Bauherrn, stießen in der Öffentlichkeit aber auf wütenden Protest. Als der Architekt sein Konzept zum ersten Mal der „Commission des Monuments Historiques" präsentierte, wurde er derart heftig angegriffen, dass seine Übersetzerin in Tränen ausbrach. Pei war nach dem Studium der Nutzerwünsche und der Erkundung des Altbaus zu der Einsicht gekommen, dass sich das Erforderliche unmöglich hinter den Fassaden des Louvre unterbringen ließe, selbst wenn das Finanzministerium, wie von Mitterrand dekretiert, ausziehen würde. Er regte deshalb an, die Höfe auszuschachten und unterhalb des Cour Napoleon und des Cour Carrée all das zu versenken, wofür sich andernorts kein Platz finden ließ – Garderoben, Vortragssäle, Parkplätze. Aber Pei wollte die in der Unterwelt gewonnenen Flächen auch nutzen, um die weit voneinander entfernten Flügel des Schlosses kurzzuschließen und einen zentralen Zugang zum Louvre zu schaffen.

conclusion that what needed to be done could not be accommodated behind the facades of the Louvre, even if the finance ministry moved out as Mitterand had decreed. He therefore proposed digging out the courtyards and burying beneath the Cour Napoléon and the Cour Carrée everything for which no other space could be found – cloakrooms, lecture rooms and parking space. But Pei also wanted to use the space underground to bring together the widely flung wings of the Louvre and create a central entrance to the museum.

What Pei proposed was no less than to construct – in the heart of France's sacred historical and cultural Parnassus – a pyramid of glass. A crystalline construction that sparkled by day and shone radiantly at night, in equal measure a showpiece, functional building, transparent entrance building and symbol of the innovation that had long seemed a step too far for conservation.

Beneath the transparent tent, a spacious distribution hall opens whence visitors can access all parts of the huge museum. Thanks to the copious supply of daylight, no visitor need feel he is down a mine. Passing through the pyramid, down a curving staircase into the hall and

93

14

Pei schlug nicht weniger vor, als im Herzen der historisch-kulturellen Überlieferung Frankreichs eine Pyramide aus Glas zu errichten. Eine kristalline Konstruktion, tagsüber funkelnd, nachts von innen leuchtend, gleichermaßen Schaustück wie Funktionsbau, transparenter Eingangspavillon und Symbol des Neuen, das der Denkmalpflege lange völlig unzumutbar erschien. Unter dem durchsichtigen Zelt öffnet sich eine großzügige Verteilerhalle, von der aus die Besucher in alle Teile des riesigen Museums gelangen können. Dank des reichlich einfallenden Tageslichtes muss sich kein Gast wie im Bergwerk fühlen, vielmehr bereitet der Gang durch die Pyramide, über eine freischwingende Rundtreppe hinab in die Halle und von dort wieder hinauf in die Galerien architektonisch auf das Kunsterlebnis vor. Die perfekt detaillierte Pyramide funktioniert gerade in ihrer Formenreinheit wie eine Schleuse in eine Welt jenseits des Alltags.

Ihr Erfolg ist einzigartig. Sie macht mittlerweile dem Eiffelturm als Wahrzeichen von Paris Konkurrenz, obwohl sie recht eigentlich nur das äußere Zeichen eines monumentalen Unterfangens ist, das den Grand Louvre aus einer verstaubten Kunstkammer in ein glänzendes Schatzhaus verwandelt hat. Pei öffnete Fußgängerpassagen durch die gewaltige Baumasse und nahm dem Louvre damit seinen Charakter als steinerne Barrikade im Zentrum der Stadt. Er schuf im Innern weitläufige, freilich nicht immer perfekt beleuchtete Galerien und ließ die kleineren Höfe überglasen, um dort Skulpturen aufstellen zu können, er durchlüftete die jahrhundertealte Anlage und formte daraus eine Ausstellungsmaschine, die jährlich ein paar Millionen Gäste beglückt. Der Protest von einst ist längst allgemeiner Begeisterung gewichen. Viele der ambitiösen „grands projets" aus Mitterands Erbmasse sind umstritten, der runderneuerte Louvre hingegen ist ein Triumph. Die Pariser haben ihn ins kollektive Herz geschlossen, die Touristen stehen vor der Pyramide Schlange. Ieoh Ming Pei wird das mit Befriedigung hören, doch ohne Überraschung. Denn der stets zuvorkommende ältere Herr hat nie etwas anderes erwartet.

Der immense Erfolg von Peis Museumsbauten bei Publikum und Kritik hat viele Gründe, aber entscheidend dürfte eine Qualität sein: ihre Verführungskraft. Es ist fast, als habe Pei irgendwann einmal die Denkschrift studiert, in der Karl Friedrich Schinkel und Gustav Friedrich Waagen im Juni 1828 über die Aufgaben des neuen Königlichen Museums in Berlin geschrieben hatten, es müsse „erst erfreuen, dann belehren." In Peis Formulierung klingt derselbe Gedanke mehr als hundertfünfzig Jahre später ganz ähnlich:

from there up again into the galleries is architectural preparation for the artistic experience that is to follow. In the perfection of its detail and formal purity, the pyramid functions like a lock-chamber accessing a meta-world beyond the mundane.

Its success is unique. It rivals the Eiffel Tower as a symbol of Paris, although strictly speaking it is only the external symbol of a monumental enterprise to transform the Grand Louvre from a dusty art repository into a gleaming treasure. Pei opened pedestrian passages through the massive masonry and thereby removed from the Louvre its character as a stone barricade in the middle of the city. Inside it he created spacious even if not always perfectly illuminated galleries, and had the small courtyards glazed over so that sculptures could be exhibited there. He introduced air into the centuries-old complex, making an exhibition machine of it that attracts millions of visitors every year. The initial storm of protest has long given way to universal enthusiasm. Many of the ambitious *grands projets* of Mitterand's legacy remain controversial, but the revamped Louvre is a triumph. Parisians have taken it to their collective heart, while tourists queue at the door of the pyramid. Ieoh Ming Pei will be pleased to hear that, but not surprised. Because the always obliging elderly gentleman never expected anything else.

There are many reasons for the immense success of Pei's museum buildings among public and critics alike, but one quality stands out: their seductive appeal. It is almost as if Pei had taken to heart the memorandum written by Schinkel and Gustav Friedrich Waagen in June 1828 about the role of the new royal museum in Berlin – it needed 'first to delight, then to instruct'. The same idea comes across in Pei's words more than a century and a half later. Museums, he once said, are not memorials. Their design should prompt the public to come and visit them 'for sheer enjoyment.'[5] Pei's subtlety lies in inciting visitors to wander through a building till they reach the galleries and see the exhibits. 'If you want people to come and to stay, you have to have space for them, and exciting sorts of movement within that space.'[6] How that works is probably best illustrated by looking at the East Wing of the National Gallery in Washington.

The building is constructed around the elegant nothing of a daylight-flooded atrium. Because this hall is triangular, it cannot be taken in all at once. Wherever you stand,

Museen, bemerkte er einmal, seien keine Gedenkstätten, ihr Design solle das Publikum vielmehr dazu bringen, aus „purem Vergnügen" zu kommen.[5] Peis Raffinement besteht darin, zur Wanderung durch ein Gebäude anzustiften, hin zu den Exponaten, hinein in die Galerien. „Wenn man will, dass die Leute kommen und bleiben, dann muss man Raum für sie schaffen, und aufregende Wege durch diese Räume."[6] Wie das funktioniert, lässt sich vielleicht am besten im East Wing der National Gallery in Washington studieren.

Der Bau ist um das elegante Nichts eines taghelles Atriums herumgebaut. Weil diese Halle dreieckig ist wie das ganze Gebäude, lässt sie sich nicht auf einen Blick erfassen. Wo immer man steht, sieht der Raum anders aus; das Auge findet keinen zentralen Fluchtpunkt. Stattdessen beginnt der Besucher, sich neugierig umzuschauen: hinauf zum vielfach verknoteten Fächerwerk des Glasdaches, dessen Schatten an sonnigen Tagen wie Federzeichnungen über die Wände wandern; hinaus in einen kleinen Skulpturengarten; oder in die Wipfel der Bäumchen, die dem Foyer die Anmutung eines „mediterranen Dorfplatzes" verleihen.[7] Vor allem aber suchen die Gäste, kaum das sie das Atrium betreten haben, die Angebote der Architektur zu erspähen: Wohin führen die beiden breiten Treppen? Welche Aussicht eröffnet sich wohl von den Stegen, die sich durch den Luftraum der Halle spannen? Am liebsten möchte man alles auf einmal machen: die Treppe hinaufsteigen, abtauchen in den Tunnel, der hinüberführt in den Altbau, über die Brücken schlendern oder in der Bibliothek stöbern. Indem Pei den Besuchern andeutet, was es alles zu entdecken gibt in einem Haus, ohne dessen Geheimnisse ganz zu entschleiern, setzt er die Massen in Bewegung. Und indem er ihnen viele Wege und Aussichtspunkte anbietet, verleiht er dem Gang durchs Museum den Charakter einer heiteren Expedition in die Welt der Kunst.

the room looks different – the eye never finds a central resting point. Instead, the visitor begins to look around with curiosity – up to the complex fan pattern of the glass roof structure, whose shadows are traced across the walls on sunny days like a moving pen drawing; out into a small sculpture garden; or to the tips of the little trees that lend the foyer the look of a Mediterranean village square.[7] But above all, visitors who have only just entered the atrium begin to succumb to the unspoken appeal of the architecture: where do the two wide staircases lead? What a view you must get from the walkways that the cross the airspace of the hall! The idea then pops up, you'd like to do everything at once – go up the steps, dive into the tunnel leading to the old building, stroll across the walkways or rummage in the library. Even while Pei is hinting to visitors – without revealing its secrets – how many things there are to discover in the building, he is getting the crowds moving. And by holding out to them the ways they can go and views they can enjoy, he lends a tour through the museum the character of a cheerful expedition into the world of art.

1   Carter Wiseman: I.M. Pei. A Profile in American Architecture, New York 1990, p. 230
2   Ieoh Ming Pei: "Museum for Chinese Art", in: Progressive Architecture 1948, p. 51
3   Walter Gropius: "Museum for Chinese Art", in: op. cit., p. 52
4   Wiseman, op. cit., p. 13
5   Gero von Boehm: Conversations with I.M. Pei, Munich 2000, p. 66
6   Ibid., p. 92
7   J. Carter Brown: "The Designing of the National Gallery of Art's East Building", in: Richard Longstreth (Ed.), The Mall in Washington, New Haven and London 1991, p. 284

1   Carter Wiseman, I.M. Pei. A Profile in American Architecture, New York 1990, S. 230
2   Ieoh Ming Pei, „Museum for Chinese Art", in: Progressive Architecture 1948, S. 51
3   Walter Gropius, „Museum for Chinese Art", in: Progressive Architecture 1948, S. 52
4   Wiseman, wie Anm. 1, S. 13
5   Gero von Boehm, „Conversations with I.M. Pei", München 2000, S. 66
6   Ebenda, S. 92
7   J. Carter Brown, „The Designing of the National Gallery of Art's East Building", in: Richard Longstreth (Ed.), The Mall in Washington, New Haven and London 1991, S. 284

Projektdaten · Project data

Bauherr · Client:
Bundesrepublik Deutschland, Bundesministerium für Verkehr, Bau- und Wohnungswesen, Bundesamt für Bauwesen und Raumordnung

Architekt · Architect
Ieoh Ming Pei, New York

Projektarchitektin · Project architect:
Christiane Flasche mit/with
Eller+Eller Architekten, Düsseldorf/Berlin

Planungstermine · Project stages:
Entwurfsbeginn · Design begin: 1996
Baubeginn · Construction begin: 1998/99
Fertigstellung · Completion: 2003

© Prestel Verlag, Munich · Berlin · London · New York, 2003

Auf dem Umschlag: Ausstellungsbau des DHM, Außenansicht ·
Cover: Exhibitions Building of the German Historical Museum, exterior view
S. 1: Terrasse im zweiten Obergeschoss (siehe S. 13); S. 2: Eingangsbereich im Erdgeschoss · Page 1: Terrace on the second floor (see p. 13);
Page 2: Entrance area on the ground floor

Die Deutsche Bibliothek verzeichnet diese Publikation in der Deutschen Nationalbibliografie; detaillierte bibliografische Daten sind im Internet über http://dnb.ddb.de abrufbar
The Deutsche Bibliothek holds a record of this publication in the Deutsche Nationalbibliografie; detailed bibliographical data can be found under: http://dnb.ddb.de

The Library of Congress Control Number: 2003105921

Prestel Verlag
Königinstrasse 9
D-80539 Munich
Tel.: +49 (89) 38 17 09-0
Fax: +49 (89) 38 17 09-35
info@prestel.de
www.prestel.de

Prestel Publishing Ltd.
4 Bloomsbury Place
London, WC1A 2QA
Tel.: +44 (20) 7323 5004
Fax: +44 (20) 7636 8004

Prestel Publishing
900 Broadway, Suite 603
New York, N.Y. 10003
Tel.: +1 (212) 995 2720
Fax: +1 (212) 995 2733
www.prestel.com

Prestel books are available worldwide. Please contact your nearest bookseller or one of the above addresses for information concerning your local distributor.

Translated from the German by Paul Aston, Dorset

Lektorat · Editorial direction: Frauke Berchtig
Copy-editing: Curt Holtz
Gestaltung und Herstellung · Design and layout: Meike Sellier
Lithografie · Origination: ReproLine, Munich
Printed and bound by Print Consult, Munich

Printed in the Slovak Republic on acid-free paper
ISBN 3-7913-2861-1

Abbildungsnachweis · Picture credits

Die Autoren · The Authors

Ulrike Kretzschmar M.A., seit 1987 im DHM tätig, ab 1991 Abteilungsleiterin Ausstellungen und Baureferentin · Ulrike Kretzschmar has been the architectural advisor and head of exhibitions at the German Historical Museum since 1991

Prof. Dr. Hans Ottomeyer, seit 2000 Generaldirektor des DHM · Hans Ottomeyer has been Director of the German Historical Museum since 2000

Prof. Dr. Werner Sewing, lehrt Architektursoziologie und -theorie an der Universität der Künste, Berlin · Werner Sewing lectures on architectural sociology and theory at Berlin's Universität der Künste

Prof. Dr. Christoph Stölzl, von 1987–1999 Gründungsdirektor des DHM · Christoph Stölzl was the founding director of the German Historical Museum from 1987–99

Dr. Heinrich Wefing, Architekturkritiker bei der *Frankfurter Allgemeinen Zeitung* · Heinrich Wefing is an architectural critic for the national newspaper, the *Frankfurter Allgemeine Zeitung*